Books for
Teachers

series editor
ALAN MALEY

THE INTERNET AND YOUNG LEARNERS

Gordon Lewis

OXFORD
UNIVERSITY PRESS

OXFORD
UNIVERSITY PRESS

Great Clarendon Street, Oxford OX2 6DP

Oxford University Press is a department of the University of Oxford. It furthers the University's objective of excellence in research, scholarship,and education by publishing worldwide in

Oxford New York

Auckland Bangkok Buenos Aires Cape Town Chennai Dar es Salaam Delhi Hong Kong Istanbul Karachi Kolkata Kuala Lumpur Madrid Melbourne Mexico City Mumbai Nairobi São Paulo Shanghai Singapore Taipei Tokyo Toronto

with an associated company in Berlin

Oxford and *Oxford English* are registered trade marks of Oxford University Press in the UK and in certain other countries

Photocopying

ISBN 0 19 442182 1

Printed in China

Acknowledgements

I would like to thank Ada Sandoval of Berlitz Kids Mexico, Laurie Camargo of Berlitz Kids Germany, and all their teachers for taking the time to review the manuscript and test the activities in their classrooms. Further thanks go to Silvana Ramponi for her comments and worksheet ideas, and Simon Murison-Bowie for being a supportive and insightful editor. My great appreciation also goes out to Julia Sallabank for believing in this project, keeping it moving, and giving me the confidence to be creative.

Finally I would like to thank my children, Kira-Sophie and Nicholas, and their friends at Tollgate School in Pennington, New Jersey, for trying out some of the activities in Spanish and giving me their honest opinions, as only children can.

Line drawings by Ann Johns.

This book is dedicated to my wife Katja.
I love her and without her nothing would have
been possible.

Contents

The author and series editor

Gordon Lewis earned a B.Sc. in Languages and Linguistics from Georgetown University, Washington D.C. and a Masters from the Monterey Institute of International Studies, Monterey, California.

While working as a freelance journalist in Vienna, Austria, he taught English and was editor of an English language cultural magazine. He founded Lewis Languages children's programme in 1991 in Berlin. In 1998 he moved to Munich to concentrate on curriculum design, materials development, and teacher training. He is co-author of *Games for Children*, also in this series.

From 2001 to 2003 he was Director of Instructor Training and Development for Berlitz Kids in Princeton, New Jersey. He is currently a freelance teacher, trainer, and materials writer, and is also on the committee of the IATEFL Young Learners Special Interest Group where he works as co-coordinator for events. In 2002 he organized a large YL Conference in Bonn, Germany.

Alan Maley worked for the British Council from 1962 to 1988, serving as English Language Officer in Yugoslavia, Ghana, Italy, France, and China, and as Regional Representative in South India (Madras). From 1988 to 1993 he was Director-General of the Bell Educational Trust, Cambridge. From 1993 to 1998 he was Senior Fellow in the Department of English Language and Literature of the National University of Singapore, and from 1999 to 2003 he was Director of the Graduate Programme at Assumption University, Bangkok. He is currently a freelance consultant. He has written *Literature*, in this series, *Beyond Words*, *Sounds Interesting*, *Sounds Intriguing*, *Words*, *Variations on a Theme*, and *Drama Techniques in Language Learning* (all with Alan Duff), *The Mind's Eye* (with Françoise Grellet and Alan Duff), *Learning to Listen* and *Poem into Poem* (with Sandra Moulding), *The Language Teacher's Voice*, and *Short and Sweet*.

Foreword

Perhaps the aptest metaphor for the Internet is the jungle. The jungle provides an endless source of sustenance and delight to those who know their way in it. To those who do not, it is a dark and impenetrable maze, full of danger and unpredictable menace. In like manner, the Internet offers infinite resources to those who can navigate its limitless pathways. For those unfamiliar with it however, it can be a threatening presence, characterized by total lack of structure, full of potential predators.

In order to make best use of the Internet's resources, those teachers unfamiliar with it need reassurance. This reassurance may be in the form of what to do and where to go to find what they are looking for. They also need to be reassured that they, and their learners (especially young learners), will be safe from some of the less palatable dangers lurking in the Internet, and to know that they can harness it to their pedagogical purposes in ways appropriate to the age and level of their learners.

This book offers precisely this kind of reassurance. It begins with a series of practical activities to familiarize learners (and teachers too perhaps!) with the way the Internet works. It moves on to activities involving communication via email. The third section offers activities to do with retrieving information from the Internet. Finally, there are activities designed to help learners build their own websites. The activities are clearly described and user-friendly, and will go a long way towards dispelling the misgivings many teachers feel about computers and the Internet as a resource.

In addition there is a rich array of useful Internet addresses. This is backed up by the book's own website (accessed via the Resource Books for Teachers site *http://www.oup.com/elt/teacher/rbt*), which is regularly updated.

Much has been made of the power of information technology in language education. This has occasionally led to a blind enthusiasm for technology without a corresponding concern for its appropriate use. This book will certainly help redress this imbalance. It views the Internet as a learning resource, to be used judiciously alongside other resources, rather than as a miracle-working solution to all learning problems. This is greatly to be welcomed.

Alan Maley

Introduction

Who is this book for?

This book is for anyone teaching English to young learners interested in enhancing their courses through the use of the Internet. The book does not assume sophisticated knowledge of computers or programming. It is not a technical how-to manual. Anybody with a general knowledge of basic word processing and web navigation can use these activities in the classroom. For those teachers with strong computer skills, the activities can serve as a creative stimulus to build impressive e-projects and tasks.

This book is obviously also for children, even if indirectly. It is for students of English between the ages of 7 and 15, though it may well be found useful for older learners, too. The activities in this book are not aimed at complete beginners. While it would certainly be possible to work with such children, this book sees the Internet as a place where we can apply our existing knowledge of the world—even expand it—but not a place to introduce new language concepts. It is not impossible to work with beginners on the Internet, but one must question whether the effort will add any value to the course being taught.

Why use the Internet?

The Internet is here to stay. Already today, children are learning Internet skills just as they learn basic reading and writing. It is common to see children already familiar with computers helping their teachers get started. The language of the Internet (or 'CyberEnglish') is an important medium in international communication. Leaving aside the pros and cons of this form of English, children must be educated to be what many people call 'electronically literate'. Since being electronically literate means not only acquiring technical skills, but also working with English, the EFL teacher is in a position to kill two birds with one stone.

The Internet provides children with a window on the outside world. It connects people from all corners of the earth through information on websites or shared projects. When used thoughtfully, Internet activities can promote tolerance and bring children together.

But using the Internet in the language classroom has many other tangible benefits. The multimedia possibilities allow us to introduce content in diverse ways and thus appeal to the learning styles or 'intelligences' of more children. It is also highly motivating. Information on the Internet is enormously diverse and not organized in any linear way. It can, therefore, be used to encourage independent learning and creative thinking skills, as children can make more decisions about how to approach information.

Beyond the foreign language classroom, the Internet offers intriguing possibilities for content-based EFL instruction. If you are working in a school environment, the Internet can provide English-language content on any subject taught in primary school, thus tying the language lessons to the mainstream curriculum. Consult with your colleagues teaching other core subjects and plan an integrated curriculum. They may be able, for instance, to pre-teach some core vocabulary for you. Even if the initial work is done in the mother tongue (see page 8), this will certainly help in framing your task. You will find many wonderful ideas for cross-curricular projects on the web. Section 7 includes a selection of particularly rich sites, which will be updated regularly on the book's website— see *http://www.oup.com/elt/teacher/rbt*.

What is the Internet?

But what exactly is the Internet? For most people, the World Wide Web ('the www' or just 'the web') comes to mind, the home to billions and billions of websites on virtually any subject under the sun and explorable through the use of web browsers. The www is as diverse as human experience and with its graphical interface and ability to integrate text, sound, video, and pictures in a communications environment, it is a very realistic and accessible place to find authentic information for the language classroom. Thanks to hypermedia (otherwise known as 'links') it is possible to move from one place on the web to another without having to follow a linear path. Rather like a mind map, the web can be navigated according to how an individual thinks.

This non-linear design makes the www an anarchic place. It mirrors the multiple perspectives and natural complexity of the world. Daunting enough for mature adults, this infinite collection of random and non-sequential bits of information can be scary and confusing for children who are just beginning to organize their ideas and knowledge, and to develop a 'world view'. Internet activities must therefore be firmly anchored in the children's own experiences and must be based on clear, purposeful tasks.

Defining these tasks in such an open-ended environment is a great challenge to teachers. The www has turned the search for content on its head. Today, our concern is with 'limiting' tasks—finding a beginning and an end to an activity. The infinite avenues to search and explore make it difficult for teachers to create meaningful frameworks for learning. If not guided, web searches can turn into unfocused, aimless wandering, never really getting to where you want to go. This book provides frameworks for exploiting the web in the language-learning classroom by providing teachers with activities that are clearly defined—that have a beginning, an end, and a clear language focus.

But the Internet is more than the www—or perhaps less. Email is an extremely potent tool for the language classroom that can operate totally independently of the web. In fact, as we shall see in some of the activities, it is possible to use email without even venturing past classroom communication. Chat programs allow children to communicate in real time with people from around the world through text, audio, or visual connections depending on available hardware and software. They can send a quick voice message or a colourful e-card. When tied to a website, chats and email allow for an optimal integration of information and communication. There are two reasons to be wary of chat programs, however. First there are the well-publicized risks of chat rooms being used by people with dishonourable intentions. Secondly there is the pragmatic issue of time—young learners are not likely to be able to cope with the pressures of having to compose messages in real time. The relatively calmer pace of email is likely to be more appropriate.

What the Internet is not

The Internet is not a replacement for classroom teaching. Nor is the Internet interactive unless the students and teachers choose to make it so. Around the world there appears to be a belief that the Internet can 'do' things to help the language learning process. In fact, the Internet can do nothing. Only when the Internet is combined with offline activities does it reach its enriching potential. Many of the core components of any Internet activity take place offline anyway. Most Internet classroom activities can and do have a non-Internet counterpart.

Instructional tool or motivator?

Will you use the Internet as an instructional tool or will it merely provide material to contextualize your offline lesson in an exciting and motivating way? It is important to understand this distinction, especially when working with beginners and/or very young learners. Will your children be performing language-learning tasks when online? Will they use the target language on the Internet? Or will they simply collect information to use in other activities such as slide shows or poster displays. Will they log on to a website about animals, for example, in order to look for specific information such as the animal's habitat or its size, or merely to find pictures of animals to illustrate their work with?

Simply mining the Internet for fun content and cool pictures is perfectly legitimate. After all, motivation and a positive attitude towards language learning should be an important goal of any young learners' classroom. However, this will need to be balanced against the realities of time and the requirements of a prescribed syllabus. Do you have time in your curriculum for activities not immediately related to the aims of your course? It is important not to let the technology drive the course. This may seem obvious, but it is very easy to get carried away by the 'bells and whistles' of the web with its bright pictures, sound and video.

For this reason this book focuses primarily on Internet activities with a clear language learning component which can be integrated into the broader scope of a language learning course.

The role of the mother tongue

One of the strongest arguments for using the Internet in the EFL classroom is the fact that it exposes the learner to authentic language. On the other hand, this exposure is not graded according to varying levels of language competence—unless, of course, you are working with a website designed specifically for language learning, of which there are not many for our age group. Thus, websites aimed at early primary students in terms of content will often still be too hard for EFL learners to follow because of the language demands.

Clearly, in order to make good use of authentic websites, we may need to use the children's mother tongue to explain the task and point the children in the right direction. Such targeted use of the mother tongue can help children isolate the elements of the website they need to work with and ignore unnecessary material. I like to call this 'framing the task'. The mother tongue is used to set the stage for the task, but is not involved in the task itself. A good example of this is activity 3.10, 'Currency converter', page 65. Most currency converter sites are full of complicated financial language and links to business sites. Our currency converter is, however, very simple. By explaining the key functions of the converter in the mother tongue (select currency to change, select amount of currency to be converted, select currency to receive) we prepare the children for a task rich in language practice.

As mentioned above, the content of many websites is either too difficult or far too complex for children to effectively exploit. It is worth considering, therefore, letting the children search mother tongue websites for information that they then report on in the target language using phrases taught in class. Is it not, after all, a very natural language situation to explain something from one's own culture to somebody in a foreign tongue?

Some search engines offer an instant translation of a website from one language to another. An interesting option could be for children to use an online translator to find the English word for a term from their mother tongue.

Finally, the need to use the mother tongue will depend on the unique mix of task and website. The teacher must try and match the children's cognitive level with their language level as closely as possible. With this determined, they would use as much of the target language as possible and as little of the mother tongue as is necessary to carry out the task.

Getting started

What do you need?

Essentials

1 A computer
The computer must have an operating system that can handle Internet services. Any recent version of Windows or Macintosh software is fine.

2 A good colour monitor
If possible try and use a monitor large enough to display web pages clearly for groups of 4–6 children. The standard of monitors has improved greatly in recent years and it should be possible to find one with crisp colours and a fairly large screen (at least 17 inches) for a reasonable price.

3 A connection to the Internet
Many schools now have central Internet access known as LANS (local area networks). If you do not have such a network, you will need to connect your computer to a network provider via a modem. A modem is a device that enables your computer to talk to a network via a telephone line. Modems can be very slow, and it is advisable, therefore, not to get one that operates under a speed of 56K. Modems can be external (connected to your computer) or built into the computer itself. Other options are high speed Internet via ISDN, DSL, or cable connections, and broadband. There will certainly be new developments in the coming years: put simply, choose the fastest connection available at your location.

4 An Internet Service Provider
In order to connect to the Internet you must have an account with an Internet Service Provider (ISP). The company will charge you for time spent online, although increasingly service is being operated at a flat rate—for one price you can be online as long as you want. If you have a 'dial-up' service, in other words if you connect to your ISP via a telephone modem, you will also have to pay the costs of the telephone connection as well. Cable-based

systems do not have this additional cost. Your ISP will almost certainly provide you with connection software and probably automatically install a web browser (Internet Explorer or Netscape Navigator).

5 A printer

Your pupils will need printed ('hard') copies of their electronic documents to complete some of the tasks in this book. They will also want to print out any web content they have created. It is worth investing a bit of money in a printer. A printer should be fast and have a good resolution (600 dpi minimum). Laser printers create very professional looking documents, but printers with ink cartridges are also very good these days. You probably also may want to consider a colour printer, since the children will want to display their work in its full glory. Unfortunately, printing colour images can be quite time consuming unless you have a top-quality printer. It also takes a lot of ink. One solution is to have two printers: one black and white one for rough drafts, worksheets and straight text, and a colour printer for final products or if a colour picture is necessary in the task.

6 Software

Be sure to check that your 'office software'—the word-processing, spreadsheet and presentation software—is up to date and generally compatible with most computer systems. If you work with a Macintosh computer, most new software will interact easily with PC's, but older versions may not translate reliably. Most computers are delivered with 'software bundles' which include all of the above applications.

In order to create emails you must also have an email program. These are generally delivered with your computer, but you can choose from many options depending on the system you use.

If you want to create web pages, you will also need a web-editing program. These programs allow you to create web content much as you would design a page with a traditional office suite of applications. The program translates your content into HTML code, which makes knowledge of HTML unnecessary. Today, many of the office software suites include web-editing capabilities into their word-processing applications and some web browsers allow you to compose content for the Internet as well.

You will find that many additional programs needed to work with the Internet are available free online. These mini-programs are known as 'plug-ins'. Plug-ins allow you, for instance, to listen to audio, play videos and animations, or to read certain text documents. New web browsers increasingly include many plug-ins in their core package. Your computer will prompt you if it needs something the browser does not supply.

Optional but useful

1 A scanner

A scanner is an incredibly useful tool for your classroom. Working much like a photocopier, a scanner reads an image and converts it into an electronic document that you can manipulate and place on a web page. This allows you to present student work (photographs, artwork and so on) and can eliminate the need for a digital camera. When buying a scanner you should pay attention to resolution. As with printers, you will need a minimum of 600 dpi.

2 A digital camera

Although a scanner can provide you with the images you need, some originals may not be that simple to scan; results may appear muddled or unclear. Having a digital camera eliminates this problem. Digital cameras also allow for immediate viewing and deletion of photographs without using up expensive film. Thus experimenting with different options becomes less cost intensive. Be sure that your digital camera has high enough resolution to produce pictures that look good on paper as well as on screen. It is also advisable to have an LCD display on the camera for children to view the photographs they take. Another important consideration is the format in which the camera saves images. If possible, get a camera that can save images as jpeg, tiff or gif files; these are the common ones.

3 A computer projector

Connecting your computer to a projector allows you to display what is on your computer monitor on to a large screen in much the same one would present a slide show. Projectors are rather expensive and an alternative is to connect your computer to a large television. Most recent television models allow for such connections.

The Internet classroom environment

Clearly, one of the major impediments to working with the Internet is the lack of a sufficient number of computers. In fact, many of us will be working in a one-computer environment. While this limits our options, it does not rule out integrating the Internet into our classrooms. Here are some things to consider:

1 Connect your computer to a projector or television screen so the whole class can view the screen and what is going on. (See the paragraph above.) This is also a very good idea in a multiple-computer environment since it allows you to explain key concepts to the entire class before breaking up into project teams. Children can also use the projector/television option to present the results of their work.

2 Most of the activities in this book have steps that can be done offline either in preparation or in summation. In planning, be sure to consider both *pre-computer* and *post-computer* work.

In many schools, access to computers is limited and children will need to be well prepared to make the most of the short time they will have online. Where computers are in short supply, instead of breaking up the class into small self-contained groups working parallel to each other, you can work with the whole class and assign different steps of an activity to individual groups—one of the steps being at the computer.

3   If you have a multi-age or mixed-ability classroom, you can assign computer work to one group of children while you focus directly on another, thus allowing for differentiated instruction. The computer becomes a workstation.

4   If all else fails, you can always create a hard-copy version of many of the activities in this book. In this scenario, you can:
   – conduct searches on your own and distribute printouts of relevant web pages to your pupils
   – collect email messages and post them for your pupils and print out replies they receive
   – collect any text, art or formatting of web pages and upload it to a website yourself. You can then either display the results via a projector or print out the web pages for the children.

5   Whether you have one computer or many in your classroom, set up a computer corner. Make it a pleasant light environment and keep it tidy and clean. This could be a task for your pupils. As you teach the language of computers and the Internet, you may want to create instructional posters to hang up in the computer corner, with tips and definitions. You can also do this in a language lab.

A model for using the Internet

Learning purposes

The first step in harnessing the Internet for classroom use is to clearly define its applications. In the young learners' environment we can break this down into three distinct areas:

– pure communication
– searching for information
– producing content for the Internet.

Pure communication

This relates to the use of email or chat programs. Using email is much like writing a normal letter, but its immediate delivery is a great motivator. Working with email is an asynchronous task—that is to say, the communication is not immediate as in a face-to-face conversation or a telephone call. It allows children time to formulate ideas, yet once they have written their response they can send it immediately. Synchronous tasks such as 'chats' occur in real-time, which means that the participants must all be online at the same time. This is obviously difficult if the chat involves people from across the world and different time zones. The dangers of chats have already been mentioned. Chats also require quick responses from learners if they are to be effective. This is a real challenge for young learners who are just beginning to learn a language; they generally need time to reflect before responding in the target language. Of course, children can take their time in responding, but then email would seem more appropriate since answers can be formulated offline and then sent. This saves money and class time. (Children can even formulate email responses as homework assignments.)

Email is fully integrated into many websites and learners do not even have to open a web browser. It can carry any number of information formats through the attachment feature. One of the great features of email is its ability to send one letter to multiple addresses. Thus, with a click of the mouse, one core activity is duplicated for the entire class. There is no end to the possibilities of what content you can introduce in these activities.

Because of its simplicity, working with email seems a good place to start. Section 2 of this book presents some very basic activities that use email.

Searching for information
The next step up from pure communication is searching for information. This normally requires the use of a web browser. At the beginning you may choose to give the children a list of pre-selected web addresses (URLs) to choose from. This will eliminate the need to operate the web browser and it will help narrow the focus of a child's exploration. Once the children are comfortable in the website environment, you can introduce them to search engines. There are many search engines geared exclusively to children. See 'Search engines: children-specific' in section 7, page 110, for a list of some good examples.

We have created a website to accompany this book, which can be accessed via the Resource Books for Teachers series website at *http://www.oup.com/elt/teacher/rbt*. Here you will find a list of regularly-updated links.

Producing content
Once the children feel confident in the web environment it is a small step to get them to begin producing their own content. In a sense they will have already done this when working with email. Now, however, they have the chance to enhance their work with all the exciting multimedia options the web has to offer (and which you are prepared to research and understand). Fortunately, basic web authoring has become quite easy through automated programs; there is no need to learn the programming language most commonly used to create web pages, HTML.

A logical bridge between searching for information and creating content is the creation of a class website. A class website can be used to practise web basics in a controlled environment. It can integrate email, and searchable web addresses can be set up as links instead of handouts. The class website can be the jump-off point for all other activities on the net, be they searches, e-contacts, projects or anything else. In a sense, the class homepage can be a multi-faceted portfolio of class work over the course of the year. It can, of course, contain the portfolios of individual children as well. See section 5, 'Electronic portfolios' and the book's website for an example.

Of course childrens' portfolios are very personal documents and not every child will feel comfortable letting anybody read them. It may therefore be advisable to limit access to these personal portfolios by adding password protection to the web pages. Most web editors allow you to define user groups and privileges, and to assign passwords. See the manual for your specific web-editing application for more details.

For more on producing content, see the sections on 'Working with e-groups and discussion lists' (page 18) and 'Weblogs' (page 19).

Preparing children for the Internet task

If your children are familiar with basic computing and web navigation, they will still need to be introduced to the specific activity you have chosen for them. In other words, you have to explain to them what you want them to do. As with any other classroom activity, the underlying task must be conceptually appropriate for the age group. Have the children learned basic research skills? Can they classify objects or recognize patterns? Can they follow directions with a series of steps? Do they have knowledge of the world, countries and customs? Can they organize their ideas in a logical order? Do they understand basic measurement concepts?

To try and answer these questions for each target age group would go well beyond the scope of this book. Deciding on an age recommendation was the most difficult part of writing the activities. Are the language needs over the head of the children or is the task itself too challenging? Sometimes it is hard to keep the two apart. In writing this book, I have tended towards challenging learners in the belief that if children can perform a task type in their mother tongue, they have the potential to do the same in the target language, provided the content they are working with is geared to their language level. As with anything new, children will need time to adjust to the Internet and to the tasks at hand.

Be patient

Children will need a lot of support at the outset, but the experience they get in one website activity is often transferable to another. It gets easier with time. With growing confidence in manipulating the Internet itself, children will be able to focus more on the language of the task.

Many problems that arise in working with the Internet can be avoided by a careful selection of websites for the task. Let's face it, this can be fairly time-consuming. Moreover, websites frequently disappear so the process of selection has to be an ongoing one. Also, you may want to customize your site selection to appeal more directly to the needs of your students. See the sections on selecting websites and creating web directories below.

Be explicit

As in most language learning activities, the more explicit you are in your instructions, the easier it will be for children to understand the task. Don't let them wander aimlessly around on a website. Guide them to the information. Limit options. Be specific in your links. Don't simply log on to a general homepage of a site if you can direct the children to the exact page they need. Older children may be capable of more open-ended searches, but children of 8–10 may well find it difficult to navigate through large sites.

Isolate the task

Some websites are full of confusing information. Currency converter sites, for example, are often packed with links to financial services. This needn't inhibit us as long as we can direct the children to the currency converter itself, which they can easily manipulate. As the Internet becomes more commercial you and the children may be confronted with a disturbing array of advertisements in the form of blinking sidebars and annoying 'pop-ups', new windows which appear when you access a site. You must teach the children to ignore these nuisances and focus on the specific task at hand.

Introducing topic and task

Before you go online with the children you need to take some time to introduce the topic you will be working on. Here are some suggested steps:

Pre-computer
– Introduce the title of the Internet task and ask the children to *predict* what it might be about.
– Ask them what they already know about the subject. Write down their ideas on the board.
– Introduce new vocabulary or review previous knowledge as it relates to the upcoming task.

Orientation
– Log on to the selected website or hand the children screenshots of the web page.
– Ask the children to scan the page for keywords.

– Let them explore the page, looking for hotlinks.
– In groups, have the children try and make mind maps of the site.

Demonstration
The easiest way for children to understand a task is to do it with them first. If you have a projector, they can follow your steps on screen. Otherwise provide them with a series of screenshots to refer to.

Circulate and help
When the children are just starting on a new web activity, you will need to monitor their progress and provide support. They can help each other too. This is a strong argument for working in groups rather than at individual terminals. Internet tasks can strengthen cooperative learning skills. Monitor group work closely to ensure that each child gets a chance to use the keyboard and mouse. It is very easy for one child to dominate.

Some practical issues

Selecting websites

Here are a few criteria to help you choose sites for use with young learners. Remember to check each site thoroughly before making your decision.

Look for simple sites with interesting graphics
Too much text will scare off young language learners. Bright colours and interesting illustrations will catch their attention. However, too many 'bells and whistles' on a page (such as animation and sound) may confuse them.

Look for sites that load quickly
Not many teachers will have the benefit of a high speed Internet connection so loading times can be long—and nothing can kill an Internet language learning class and demotivate your children quicker than a slow-loading site. Again, look for simple sites without intricate plug-ins or elaborate audio and visual options.

Look for sites with clear and easy navigation
Once on a site, you want children to be able to get to the information as quickly and efficiently as possible. Simple homepages with a site map or guide are ideal for children. If possible, the navigation should be iconic—in other words, links should be in the form of pictures, with titles written underneath. In moving from page to page, it is advisable to observe a 'two click rule': after logging on to a website, it should not take you more than two clicks of the mouse to get to real content. In the case of the activities in this book, it means that as a rule of thumb, the answers or information should be no more than two clicks away.

Be sure you know who is behind your site
The Internet is not a controlled environment and there is always the potential that dishonest people will use a website as bait to lure people for their own ends. Some apparently innocent sites are actually fronts for religious or other organizations interested in collecting data on people visiting the homepage. You can avoid this by choosing sites managed by well-established organizations or those you are already familiar and comfortable with. You may want to check the appropriacy of the advertizing, too.

Creating a web directory

'You never know where you're going till you get there.' This couldn't be truer than when talking about the Internet. Altering one word in a search box can send you to a completely different place. Soon you find yourself in a totally unexpected corner of Cyberspace and if you don't keep track of your steps, you may never be able to get back there again. For this reason it makes good sense to start building a web directory from the very start of your work with the Internet. This is extremely easy—a click of a menu item. If you are using Internet Explorer, you create a list of 'Favourites'. If your browser is Netscape Navigator, the list will be called 'Bookmarks'. These are two words for the same thing: the web addresses (URLS) of sites you have visited and that you may wish to visit again.

Bookmarks and Favourites can quickly and easily be organized into folders so that you can find them more easily. You can even 'publish' these collections of links on your school or class web page and thereby control and limit the 'surfing' your students do. Free programs available on the Internet can also combine all your Bookmarks or Favourites on to one 'page' for easier use.

Web browsers also offer you a built-in option to retrace your steps: the menu item 'History'. This feature documents all of your movements on the WWW over a period of time. You can set the duration you desire (one day, two days, a week): with Internet Explorer, for example, this is done by clicking on 'Tools' then 'Internet options'. While the History feature cannot sort links as Favourites or Bookmarks can, it is very valuable should your computer crash.

Contacting partners

If you plan to develop an e-partnership with another institution either abroad or locally, you must begin making contacts long before your class project starts. You will need to explain your project and place it on one of the many international databases or 'listserves' where like-minded educators post their own ideas or search for partners.

Once you establish initial contact you will need to discuss and agree upon the rules of your interaction and get a commitment on time frames for responses. There is nothing more frustrating for children than getting no answers to their emails. Therefore, be realistic. People have busy lives and communication tasks should be short and very focused.

See 'Finding partners' in section 7, page 110, and the book's website, for web addresses to contact partners.

Creating questionnaires and worksheets

For many activities in this book there are templates for worksheets children can use to record information from their Internet searches. You can find these at the back of the book, and on the book's website as downloadable documents. In other cases, where the content is not specified, you will have to come up with the relevant questions. A good way to make such worksheets or forms is to use the Table function in an application like Microsoft Word. There is also a huge variety of activity generators available free on the web; these allow you to create games, quizzes and worksheets. This book's website has links to a few of them.

Working with e-groups and discussion lists

One of the easiest ways to communicate on the Internet and share files is to create an 'e-group' or discussion list. Unlike creating a web page, which requires a fair amount of time and some basic familiarity with web tools, discussion groups have a built-in structure that you can immediately activate and start using. Unlike decentralized email that sends messages only to individual accounts, discussion lists group all postings in one place that all members of the list can access and read. This makes it easy for everybody to follow a discussion and contribute. Of course, it is also possible to have the messages on the central site sent to the individual email address as well.

One great function of e-groups is the ability to upload files to the list for every member to share. Thus, rather than creating web pages, your students could create Word documents or scan in pictures and place them as files on the group site. This might be easier for you and your students and it has the added advantage of allowing you to make content available on the web without having to find a host for your own site—a cheaper alternative for those with tight budgets.

When you create an e-group, you become a moderator and can set certain standards for the group. Some groups are very open and anyone can join. Others are more restrictive. As moderator you can set the parameters so that anyone wanting to join has to have your approval first. This is important when working with children. By keeping membership approval in your hands you can safeguard against anyone prowling your site to make contact with your children for unethical purposes. Basically, you will be checking email addresses for their authenticity. If you can't reasonably trace an email address to an identifiable user or institution, don't allow them to join. When working with partner schools, you can ask your colleagues to pre-approve their students' email addresses for membership.

Many e-groups also come equipped with built-in chat software. If you have a closed group this can be a safe option for your children to test the waters of synchronous communication. In fact, they can choose to log on to the chat individually from home and simply check if anyone else is online.

Another function that is particularly fun to use with children is the polling option. This function allows you to ask the group certain questions and members can respond in multiple-choice style, making it easy for the children to answer.

Since e-groups are free, you can create as many as you want—one per project or topic—or you can choose to keep everything in one place and simply change the discussion from time to time.

The best sites I have found for creating e-groups are listed under 'E-groups' in section 7, page 110.

Weblogs or 'blogs'

Recently many people have turned to 'blogs' as an alternative to traditional websites and discussion lists. Blogs are web diaries with built-in tools that allow users to publish information on the web in much the same way they use a text program. Unlike traditional websites, blogs are automatically updated each time a person publishes a new 'posting'. Thus, rather than you, the teacher, regularly needing to update a class website, any registered user with publishing privileges can immediately add to the site. This can obviously save you a lot of time. As moderator, you can easily determine who has publishing privileges by adjusting the blog settings. You can also, for instance, choose to view all postings before allowing them to be published on the blog—a good idea when working with young learners.

Weblogs can be private, or community-based. You can determine membership in a community group. You can create a class weblog where everyone (perhaps even parents) can contribute. You may in addition let each child set up and manage their own individual weblogs where only they can publish (subject to your approval). These private weblogs are very empowering for children. It gives them a real platform and control over what they want to say.

Since weblogs are organized chronologically, they have the potential to provide a clear record of a child's progress in English. In fact, they are a simple alternative to more elaborate portfolios (see section 5, 'Electronic portfolios', pages 101–104), involving at least basic design skills.

Unlike discussion list postings, blog postings can contain pictures, audio/video files and links in the body of the message. The only issue here is that you must have some place to store any images or audio you choose to integrate. They can either be displayed in the body of the message or simply shown as links. Most free blogging sites will only host text-based blogs, but you can link to images elsewhere on the web even though you cannot upload images or audio files to the free site.

For more more information on blogs, see 'Weblogs' in section 7, page 112, and the book's website.

Internet safety

As noted above, the Internet is a mirror of the real world and this includes potential dangers—not limited to the use of chat rooms. The content on the Internet is not screened by any central authority and thus it is possible that children can access material that is not appropriate for their age group (or any age group for that matter!). Similarly, the anonymity of the Internet means that communication via email has its risks.

The best approach to guaranteeing Internet safety is to keep a sharp eye out for what is going on in the classroom. It is unwise simply to allow the children to work freely online. As you will see below, the activities in this book are all designed to limit such random 'surfing', but you must actively monitor computer work.

Of course, you can't be everywhere at once. Using child-safe search engines will also help protect your children from inappropriate material. These search engines pre-select sites for their suitability for children. You will find a list of the most popular child-safe search engines under 'Search engines: children-specific' in section 7, page 111.

In addition to search engines, you can also limit random searching by using 'web filters'. Many online services and web browsers have built in 'parental controls' which scan websites and block access if they have questionable content. In addition to these built-in filters, you can also purchase more powerful web filters, which you can adjust to suit your individual needs. All of them are very easy to set up and use.

Email and chat rooms probably pose an even greater threat to children's security. Online predators have been known to establish contact with children and coax personal information from them or arrange live meetings, which can be extremely dangerous. Take some time to establish a set of 'Internet rules' with your students, just as you establish rules for your classroom as a whole. Display the rules in the classroom prominently. Be clear how serious these rules are. Maybe ask your children to sign an *Internet Code of Conduct*.

Here are some of the key rules to follow:

– Never allow the children to divulge any private information such as address or telephone number.
– Monitor email and allow the children only to send email to addresses you have already approved (such as in school exchanges). Some Internet services will allow all emails sent by the children to be copied to the teacher's email account. See if your provider has this option.
– Do not allow children to open emails from an unknown source.
– If an unknown email arrives, the children must report it to the teacher.
– All material published by the children on the Internet must be approved by the teacher and the parents.

Many students also have Internet connections at home. It is a good idea to send the Internet rules to the parents to read and enforce. They may not be aware of the inherent dangers of online work.

Viruses

Being connected to the WWW can expose your computer to viruses, aggressive computer programs that can destroy your data or erase your hard disk. Viruses come in all shapes and sizes and are often transported as attachments to emails. Be very careful when opening email attachments from unknown sources. You can set your email program to block certain messages or 'quarantine' them until you decide they are safe.

There are many anti-virus applications commercially available. These applications are being constantly updated, but malicious programmers are always one step ahead. Don't rely on anti-virus applications to protect you—be on your guard.

Copyright issues

In principle, Internet content enjoys the same copyright protection as material available in more traditional forms such as books or videos. With all copyright works there is a general principle of 'fair use', though the principle is not clearly defined. What constitutes fair use will depend on the individual materials you and your students want to use and how you intend to use them.

In general, using copyright-protected material as part of an educational project is considered 'fair use'. The web creation activities in this book all fit this definition. In other words, it is all right for children to cut and paste images and other materials from websites as long as they adhere to certain limitations. These limitations differ from media to media (audio, video, text, etc.), but as a rule of thumb, you and your students should not copy more than 10 per cent of content without asking for permission. If you are copying entire sections of websites and using them in their original form, you may be breaking 'fair use' principles. These guidelines apply not only to student work, but to teacher websites and portfolios as well.

If you intend to use any of the copied material commercially, no matter what percentage of content, you must seek permission. If in doubt, always ask, before you get into legal difficulties.

How to use this book

The book and its website

This book is accompanied by its own website, to be found at *http://www.oup.com/elt/teacher/rbt*. In the rapidly changing world of the Internet it is quite impossible to ensure that all the links mentioned in the body of the book and more particularly in section 7, 'Useful Internet addresses', are up to date. You should, therefore, keep an eye on what is happening on the book's website. Here you will find not only new links but also a glossary of technical terms, downloadable versions of the worksheets in the book as well as new ones, and a place where you can express your views about the book. There is also the opportunity for children to post their own work, and to look at the work of others. So the first way to use this book is in conjunction with the website.

How the book is organized

The main part of this book is its four sections of activities. Section 1 consists of a small number of activities to familiarize children (and teachers?) with basic computer and Internet skills. Section 2 focuses on using the Internet as a means of getting children to communicate with other children around the world. Section 3 offers a wide range of activities that involve children in searching the web for information to support their learning and give them insight into other people's lives. Section 4 concentrates on activities that will have children creating their own websites, working with e-groups and taking part in online discussions.

How each task is organized

Each task is organized according to the following categories:

Level

The level given indicates the *minimum* language required to complete the task. It does not refer to a child's overall cognitive level, which is better reflected by the age recommendation. Many activities can be adjusted to the appropriate language levels by tailoring the content of the task. The language levels used are:

Beginner

Children at this level are just starting to learn English. They can use the language for very basic communication purposes. They understand the verb *be* and the modal *can* as well as *do*, *wh-* questions, basic commands and key formulaic phrases. They recognize basic vocabulary relating to topics such as *family*, *animals*, *colours*, *numbers*, etc.

Elementary

Children here have a more active grasp of the content at the beginner level. They can talk about people and places and describe actions. They can make comparisons, express possession, talk about time, use the simple past tense, the present simple and present progressive tenses, and basic prepositions. They have a more diversified range of vocabulary including topics such as food, transportation, and clothes.

Pre-intermediate

Children at the pre-intermediate level have the ability to express basic needs, ideas, and desires in English. They can use more complex sentences with conjunctions such as *but* or *because*. They can also talk about degree (*how tall?*) and frequency (*sometimes*, *never*).

Intermediate and above

Intermediate children can express themselves independently in English. Most children at this level will be older (over 10). They can talk about recent events and experiences (present perfect) and the future (*will/going to*) in addition to the material at the previous levels. At this level children can talk about any age-appropriate subject and have the skills to find vocabulary if they don't know the words themselves.

Age

Alongside the difficulty of learning English, the Internet also places broader cognitive demands on the children. Internet tasks must, therefore, be carefully aligned to the developmental level of the children. Children in the early primary years are still learning basic concepts and will not be able to perform certain complicated tasks.

Particular attention must be paid to research skills. It is extremely difficult for fledgling primary school children to pick out key information on a very busy page. Therefore, any web searches must closely guide the children through extraneous material and take them directly to the place the key information can be found.

Just as we can adjust the language level, so too can we modify many tasks to match the developmental level of the children. We can even differentiate Internet activities to account for mixed abilities within the individual class itself.

Many Internet activities support learning across the curriculum. It is, therefore, important to be aware of what children are learning in their other subjects. What mathematical concepts have they learned? Have they developed certain reading strategies? What have they covered in basic science classes? If you work at a school, consult with your colleagues. If you are in a private situation, get hold of the local school curriculum, which will in most cases outline the skills and concepts being taught at each grade level.

Time

Times indicated are minimum times for working through each activity. Most activities will have online and offline time. While the online time is relatively predictable, the offline component can vary greatly depending on the language level of the children. Many activities are 'ongoing' and have no time restrictions at all.

Depending on the situation you teach in, you may have to work in varying time-blocks (45 minutes, 1 hour, 90 minutes). You will need to break down the activities accordingly.

In my experience, Internet activities take longer than expected. Be prepared for slow connections that make loading websites take a long time.

Aims

Each activity is designed to engage young learners with the Internet and its various media by setting one or more tasks with clear learning aims. These aims are expressed in a variety of ways: as a communicative function, as a skill to be practised, or as specific language to be used. In all cases language use is at the core of the activity even though it may not be the object of the lesson.

Language
Here you will find key phrases and vocabulary that the learners will either be exposed to or use in the activity. In most of the activities there is, however, a high degree of flexibility. Where the activity is very dependent on specific input, the language component may only be a function or skill, with the content vocabulary to be determined by the individual teacher. Many activities are also multi-purpose and can be used as frameworks to introduce any number of language items, making them very flexible and convenient for teachers.

As mentioned earlier, the Internet is not a medium to introduce new language, but rather one where we can apply existing knowledge and skills in a motivating context. Before beginning many Internet activities it will be necessary to pre-teach relevant vocabulary and structures.

Materials

This includes everything which you need to prepare for the task.

Preparation

This indicates what you need to do before the class. Often it involves you in familiarizing yourself with a particular website so that you can be confident in helping the children find their way round in the most effective ways.

In class

This is a step-by-step guide to what you do in class. You will certainly want to adjust the suggestions to fit your own teaching style and your children's needs.

Variations

These are more ideas and suggestions for modifying or extending the activity. Adapt and experiment to make the activity your own.

Comments

These provide background information on the activity to help you make best use of the activity in the classroom.

Offline versus online steps

I have not broken down the steps of each activity into pre-computer, online and post-computer segments. Nevertheless, it is important for you to take this into consideration when planning your lessons. You will find it easy to distinguish between online and offline steps.

Depending on whether you have in-class computers or time in a computer lab, you may want to break up the activities: you can prepare the offline steps in one lesson and go online in the computer room in another. In this way, even those of you with few computer skills can successfully set up Internet activities in class and perhaps team up with a computer specialist (or simply a technically-minded colleague) for the online segment.

1 First steps

This first section of activities is designed to help you make sure that your children are sufficiently familiar with computers and the things that go with them to be able to do the other activities in the book. It may well be that your children are completely at ease with computers and the Internet. If this is so, go straight on to the rest of the book.

You can use this section as a checklist of necessary computing skills and, unlike the other sections, the activities here are graded. They start with the most basic knowledge and then look at increasingly sophisticated skills. However, activity 1.2, 'Typing practice', is a bit different. To get started, children need at least to be able to pick out the relevant keys without too much difficulty. Typing is a skill that requires a lot of practice and you may consider making this a regular feature of your classroom work. See this activity's Comments for more on this.

You may care to use the following inventory of computer and Internet skills to check your children's ability. The activities which follow can be used diagnostically—there are few children who will readily admit to not knowing absolutely everything about computers—and then used more extensively to plug any holes in their abilities.

To benefit most from the activities in this book, children will need to know:

– the main components of a computer and the main features of its 'desktop' (activity 1.1)
– how to use the keyboard (activity 1.2)
– how to use scroll bars (activity 1.3)
– how to use the mouse to click on an object and to 'drag and drop' (activity 1.4)
– how to cut and paste text and illustrations from one document to another (activity 1.5)
– how to open a computer application
– how to save documents
– how to use pull-down menus to format documents (fonts, colours, etc.)
– how to identify the navigation of a browser (back arrow and forward arrow, address bar), identify a web address and move around the computer screen and recognize 'hotlinks' (activity 1.6)
– how to understand key commands in an email program.

1.1   Computer objects

LEVEL

Beginner and above

AGE

7 and above

TIME

40 minutes

AIMS

To identify the various components of a computer and its desktop.

Language: Computer vocabulary as on worksheet 1.1.

MATERIALS

Worksheet 1.1, 'Computer objects', one for each child.

IN CLASS

1 Ask the children if they know what a computer is. The answer will be pretty obvious.

2 Point to your computer and say: *This is my computer.* Pick up your mouse and say *and this is my mouse.*

3 Point to the printer and ask *What's this?*

4 Continue pointing out objects and eliciting responses.

5 Write the English words up on the board.

6 Hand out the copies of worksheet 1.1.

7 Ask the children to draw a line from a word to the appropriate picture.

VARIATION 1

Create a similar worksheet for the desktop of your operating system.

VARIATION 2

For children with language skills beyond the elementary level you can use an information gap activity instead of the worksheet.

1.2   Typing practice

LEVEL

Elementary and above

AGE

8 and above

TIME

Ongoing (approximately 15 minutes a session)

AIMS

To practise typing on a keyboard and remembering location of important keys.

Language: The Roman alphabet.

MATERIALS

Light pieces of fabric, large enough to cover a keyboard—one for every computer being used by the children. Small stickers with nice pictures or bright colours to stick on important keys. Flashcards with names of keys you want to introduce.

PREPARATION

Depending on your computer system, affix stickers to important keys such as:

– *enter*
– *control-alt-delete*
– *backspace*
– *apple (for Macintosh users)*
– @ (called the 'at' key)

IN CLASS

1 If possible each child in class should work on an individual computer and keyboard. If this is not possible, split the class into small groups and have the children take turns. Another alternative is to create a computer workstation and have the remaining children do other activities.

2 Ask the children to type their names into the computer.

3 Randomly ask a few of the children to spell their names out loud.

4 Introduce important keys. (See Preparation.) Demonstrate their function or explain it in the children's mother tongue.

5 Hold up flashcards with various keys on them. The children must type them. To make this more interesting for more advanced children, add a number, for example *type four @s (ats),* or hold up a picture of an object they know and ask them to spell it, for example *dog, glass, mother.*

6 When you are confident the children have a basic knowledge of the keyboard, hand out the fabric you have brought to class and instruct the children to place it over the keyboard.

7 Hold up flashcards of various keys and/or words as before. The children try to type the key with their hands under the fabric. They can check their accuracy on the screen.

8 Do this activity regularly throughout the school year for 10–15 minutes per week.

COMMENTS

Familiarizing the children with the keyboard early on will help avoid typing mistakes and give them confidence in their work. You may want to conduct this activity together with a computer or reading/writing specialist. Alternatively you might like to use a typing program; there are several available over the web—see 'Typing programs' in section 7, page 111—or simply use a search engine like Google and type in *learn typing.*

1.3   The elevator

LEVEL	**Beginner and above**
AGE	**7 and above**
TIME	**30 minutes**
AIMS	**To practise working with a scroll bar and to scan a text quickly for specific words.**
MATERIALS	A word processor, available on all computers.

PREPARATION

Create a word-processed document with the names of animals spread across many pages and seemingly at random intervals. For Variation 1, add links to local web pages you create. Make sure this document is visible on the desktop of all the children's computers. Give it the title *The elevator*.

IN CLASS

1 Split the children up into small groups around a computer screen and keyboard.

2 Ask the children to open the document titled *The elevator*, by double-clicking on its icon.

3 Demonstrate to the children how to use the scroll bar on the right hand side of the screen. Show them how to 'click and drag' through the document by clicking on the small square in the scroll bar and moving it up and down.

4 Let the children practise this skill for a short time. Then ask them to drag the square to the top of the scroll bar (the start of the document).

5 Tell the children that you are going to call out a word or phrase. They must try and find it as fast as possible. The first group to find the word or phrase should call out *Got it*. Check for accuracy.

6 All groups must let go of their mouse when someone calls *Got it*. The search resumes from the place they left off in the document.

VARIATION 1

If you have access to a local area network (LAN), you can create a series of web pages with pictures of objects, actions and people. In this variation, place links instead of words or pictures in random places in a word-processed document. The children must not only use the scroll bar, but practise opening and closing web links as well.

VARIATION 2	Rather than pictures, objects, or actions, the web pages you create could include clues to a hidden identity or any other mystery. For instance, you may be searching for an animal. Link clues could include:

– It is very large.
– It lives in Asia.
– It has orange and black stripes.

The children must move through the document, clicking on links until they feel they know the answer.

1.4 Click, drag, and drop

LEVEL	**Beginner and above**
AGE	7 and above
TIME	**30 minutes**
AIMS	**To understand and use the concept of 'drag and drop'.** **Language:** Basic prepositions of place.
PREPARATION	Clear the desktops of your children's computers so that very few objects are visible. The one object remaining should be your Internet browser icon.
IN CLASS	1 Show the children a picture of the Internet browser icon you use or point to it on your desktop if you have a computer projector.
	2 Ask the children to find it on their screen.
	3 Pick up your mouse and move it about so that the small arrow on the computer screen moves. If you don't have a projector, move among your children to be sure they see that the mouse moves the arrow.
	4 Ask the children to place the arrow on the browser icon. Check to be sure that all children have done this.
	5 Ask the children to 'click' on the icon. The icon should be highlighted. Demonstrate with your mouse. Perhaps unplug your mouse and walk about the room showing them. Write the word *click* on the board.
	6 Ask the children to move the arrow off the icon and click again. The highlighting should disappear.
	7 Practise this a few times, saying *click on*, *click off*.
	8 Ask the children to click on the icon one more time, this time not releasing the mouse button. Demonstrate on screen or bring your mouse and show the children.

9 Once the children have done this, ask them to move the mouse without letting go. The icon should move with it. Tell them to let go of the mouse button and then move the mouse again. The icon will stay where they left it.

10 Ask the children to click on the icon again and ask them to move the icon:
  – to the middle
  – to the upper right corner
  – to the lower left corner
  – to the lower right corner.

VARIATION

Instead of moving one browser icon, you can create a series of files with photos of the children or pictures of animals or any other objects you may choose. Teach the children to open a file by 'double-clicking'. Ask them to find a particular person, animal or object by opening and closing files (by checking the close box in the upper right corner of the active window). They can move the chosen file or document to be in relation to other objects on the desktop. This will give you good reason to increase the language content to add prepositions such as: *next to*, *under* and *over*.

COMMENTS

Try and have the same mouse for each work station: 'mice' vary. Be especially aware of the difference between Macintosh and Windows computers in this respect.

1.5 Cut and paste

LEVEL

Beginner and above

AGE

7 and above

TIME

30 minutes

AIM

To learn how to cut and paste images from the Internet to a word-processing document.

PREPARATION

1 Prepare a word-processing document with a table (2 columns × 5 rows: see the picture on page 34, which is also provided in downloadable form on the book's website). In each row of the left hand column write a name of an animal, object, or person— whatever suits you and your class. Be sure this document is available on all your computers or teach your children how to make the table on their own. Name the document *Cut and Paste*.

2 (optional) Create a handout with a list of websites for the children to search.

MATERIALS

Website list handout (optional).

IN CLASS

1 Ask the children to open the word-processing document.

2 Tell the children that you want them to find pictures of the words in the left column of the table and paste them into the right column.

3 Ask the children to log on to a common search engine such as Google, Altavista, Ask Jeeves, etc. (See 'Search engines: general' in section 7, page 111.) Most search engines have specific image or picture search buttons. Show the children where the button is and tell them to click on it. A new search form will appear.

4 Ask the children to type in the first word in the left column and press 'Enter'. A collection of images will appear.

5 Tell the children to place the mouse pointer over the image of their choice.

6 For Windows users, have the children click on the right mouse button and choose 'Copy' from the menu that appears. Mac users click and hold down the mouse button until a menu appears (there is only one mouse button), highlight 'Copy' and release the mouse button.

7 Ask the children to return to the word-processing document. (See your operating system help for how.)

8 Have the children click their mouse pointer in the right-hand column of the table next to the word they have selected.

9 From the 'Edit' menu of the word-processing program have the children select 'Paste'. The image they chose should appear in the table.

10 Repeat the process for the other words in the table.

VARIATION 1

Rather than using an image search on a search engine, give the children specific web addresses to search for and copy images.

VARIATION 2

If you want to practise cutting and pasting text, create a word-processing document with a one-column table. In each row of the table write a section of a simple story, but jumble the order. Have the children, highlight, cut, and paste the sections into the appropriate order.

rabbit	
bird	
lion	
giraffe	
skunk	

1.6   Finding your way on the web

LEVEL

Elementary and above

AGE

8 and above

TIME

40 minutes +

AIM

To familiarize the children with the architecture of a web browser and web pages.

MATERIALS

Worksheet 1.6, 'Finding your way on the web', one for each child.

PREPARATION

Select five or six age-appropriate fun websites with lots of hotlinks on their homepages. Put them into a single document to distribute to the children.

IN CLASS

1 Write a local address on the board, maybe the address of the school. Ask the children if they recognize it. Hand the children a list of five or six web addresses or write the addresses on the board. Tell them that there are addresses on the Internet as well. All addresses take this form, more or less.

2 Ask them to type in the first into the address bar (you may have to show them how to delete the current address by backspacing) and press 'Enter'.

3 Let them move their mouse around the web page. Do they see something happening when they move over some sections (preferably find a website where hotlinks change colour or are underlined)?

4 Let them click on a link. (Hopefully it will load quickly.)

5 Point to the address bar and show them that they are at a new address.

6 Tell them you want to go back to the previous page. With exaggerated gestures ask them how to do this? See if anyone comes up with the back and front arrows.

7 Let them click forward and backward a few times.

8 Ask the children to type in the rest of the web addresses on the sheet and browse around, following links.

9 Move around the room and help where appropriate.

10 Give each child a copy of worksheet 1.6, 'Let's navigate the Internet', to keep in their folder (or glue to the inside cover).

FOLLOW-UP

Blow up a large copy of the worksheet and display it prominently in your classroom.

1.7   What's in a website?

LEVEL

Elementary and above

AGE

8 and above

TIME

40 minutes + and ongoing

AIM

To give the children a taste of what a website contains.

MATERIALS

Worksheet 1.7, 'What's in a website?', one for each child.

PREPARATION

Select a small number of websites from the ones looked at in the previous activity. Choose sites that have interesting but simple content and which have plenty of pictures, interactivity, and hotlinks. Familiarize yourself with their contents.

IN CLASS

1 Write up the web addresses of three or four websites which you have chosen as part of your preparation.

2 Put the children in small groups to choose and explore a particular website. Encourage them to look for different kinds of content and to say what they like or dislike about the site.

3 Hand out the worksheet and get them to fill it in, either as a group or individually. If necesssary, use another website of your own choosing to demonstrate the idea of the mind map.

FOLLOW-UP

This can be an ongoing activity, especially as a preliminary to the use of a particular website that is content-rich and essential to the carrying out of the activity. Older children can be encouraged to use the approach to critique a website—to say whether they think it works well or not.

2 Communication activities

Communicating with people around the world by email can be a very exciting and motivating activity for young learners, but these interactions must be well prepared if they are not to be frustrating for children. Because email is so 'instant' children expect a quick response to emails that they send and a lack of response will be very demotivating. To ensure success, start making contacts with potential partners three months in advance of introducing the activity. This will give you time to get to know potential partners.

The easiest way to get started is to join an existing network. In this way you will be able to participate without having to organize everything yourself. You can learn from the experience of participation and then go on to launch your own project.

Most of the activities in this section can be conducted with one partner or a larger network. Although they are listed under the communication heading, almost all of the activities involve significant content creation on the part of the children.

'Finding partners' in section 7, page 110, lists some popular sites to make contacts with potential partners or join existing Internet projects.

2.1 Who am I?

LEVEL	**Elementary and above, depending on variation and region**
AGE	8 and above
TIME	45 minutes +
AIMS	**Asking for personal information.** **Language:** The verb *to be*, present simple, *wh*-questions.
MATERIALS	Email index cards.
PREPARATION	Before class you must create email accounts for your students. Many schools can assign addresses to the students directly; otherwise you can create free email addresses. (See 'Email: free services' in section 7, page 110.) Make sure the addresses you create do not include the full names of the children. (See page 20 on Internet safety.)

1 Ask the children if they know what email is. Write the word on the board. Tell them that email is like sending a letter but it is much quicker. Everybody has an email address. Write an email address up on the board. Use something obvious such as: teacher@ourschool.com. Don't worry about explaining the @ sign, or *com* or *org*. At this point you only want the children to recognize an email address.

2 Explain to the children that each of them will receive their own email address.

3 Pass out a 'secret' card to each child with the child's individual address on the top of the page and another email address listed on the bottom. It would be good to colour code the addresses and refer to 'red' address (top) and 'green' address (bottom). Do not let the children tell each other their addresses.

4 Tell the children that they must now find out who is behind the 'green' email address on their 'secret' paper by emailing and asking questions.

5 If the group is intermediate or above, let them come up with their own set of questions. If they are elementary level, you can write sentences or sentence stems on the board for them to work with. Some examples could be:

–*What colour hair do you have?*
–*Are you a boy?*
– *Do you sit next to …?*
–*Are you tall?*
–*Where do you live?*
– *Do you have a brother/sister?*

VARIATION

Instead of guessing the name of the person behind an email, give each student an animal identity. The students must ask questions and identify the animal. This version is quite good to use if you have a limited number of computers and have to work in small groups.

2.2 Getting to know you

LEVEL

Elementary and above

AGE

8 and above

TIME

30 minutes

AIMS

To elicit information about your students.

Language: Question words, personal details (varies according to individual criteria).

PREPARATION

1 Prepare a list of questions you want the children to answer. For an elementary group these questions might be:

–What is your name?
– How old are you?
– Do you have a pet?
–What are your hobbies?
– Do you like English?
–What is your favourite music?

2 Open up your email application and create a distribution list with the email addresses of all your students listed. You will be asked to name your list and then you can type in the names and addresses of your students. See the operating instructions of your email application for exact details on where to find the 'new distribution list' command.

3 Enter a greeting such as *Welcome to my class!* in the subject line of the email.

4 Write a brief introduction at the top of the mail. This could read:

Hi children! I'm your teacher, Mr/Ms___. I want to know more about you. Can you answer these questions for me? Send me an email! Thank you.
Mr/Ms —.

IN CLASS

1 Tell the class that you have sent them an email message. You want them to tell you a little bit about themselves.

2 Have the children open the message you sent. Give them some time to read it.

3 Check for comprehension.

4 If you haven't done so already, demonstrate how to reply to an email message. Give the children approximately 15 minutes to respond.

VARIATION

This activity can be used as an online assessment test or a regular review after completing a unit in the course book.

FOLLOW-UP

You can use this personal information to design activities geared to the specific interests of the class.

COMMENTS

This activity is suitable for a new class at the beginning of the year. It is a good example of one-to-many type of email communication.

2.3 Introduction to e-cards

LEVEL

Elementary and above

AGE

7 and above

TIME

40 minutes

AIMS

To identify different types of e-cards and occasions for sending them.

Language: To work with phrases related to letter writing in general and specific occasions such as birthdays, holidays, or vacations.

PREPARATION

Pre-select a list of e-card websites for the children to search and create a handout for the children. See 'E-cards' in section 7, page 109, for some suggestions.

MATERIALS

Handout with list of web addresses, a postcard with a text written by the teacher, various other cards (postcards, get-well cards, birthday cards, etc.).

IN CLASS

1 Hold up a postcard to your class. Tell the children that you received the postcard from someone on holiday. Read the text. It could be:

Dear X,
It is great here in XXX. I'm having lots of fun. I wish you were
here too.
Yours,
Y

2 Ask the children if they have ever received a postcard before.

3 Hold up the other cards you brought with you. Explain to the children that there are cards for many different occasions. Give a few examples. Elicit further examples from the children and write their ideas up on the board in English.

4 Explain to children that now you can send cards to people via the Internet. These cards are called e-cards and there are lots and lots of them to choose from.

5 Hand out the list of websites to the children. Ask them to choose a type of card to look for.

6 Split the class up into small groups and have the children log on to the Internet and explore one of the addresses on the list.

7 Tell the children to select one card to describe to the rest of the class.

COMMENTS

E-cards come in many forms. Some allow for free writing while others simply let children click on appropriate text. The final form of your e-card activity will depend on the genre and design of the card you choose. Basically, anything you write in an email can also be sent in an e-card, provided the text is not too long. Since they are bright, colourful, and fun, they are a motivating alternative to the grey email programs available elsewhere.

2.4   Finding partners

LEVEL

Pre-intermediate and above

AGE

8 and above

TIME

90 minutes

AIMS

To establish contact with a partner school in a foreign country.

Language: Present simple tense, verb *to be*, *do/don't*, vocabulary of family, town, school.

PREPARATION

Select a partner school to work with. You can find partners by searching a common school-to-school network. (See 'Finding partners' in section 7, page 110, and the book's website.) Let the children browse the entries and choose partners from around the world according to what interests them most. You can also place your own project profile on the network list. Potential partners need not be in English-speaking countries. They may be learners just like your children or attend an international school. Once you have made contact with a partner, explain the project in greater detail (including time requirements) and get a commitment of participation.

IN CLASS

1 Prepare an introductory email describing your school and town. If you have access to either a digital camera or scanner you can provide photographs or pictures drawn by the children and create a document attachment to go with the email.

2 If you are comfortable with the technology or have technological support, take a class photograph with a digital camera and create 'hotlinks' under each child's picture which connect to a personal information page that each child can design. This personal information can be very simple, such as likes and dislikes, pets and their names, etc.

VARIATION 1

Instead of hotlinks to photos of the children, scan in pictures they have drawn.

VARIATION 2

Instead of hotlinks connecting to a child's personal page, the links can open an email window where children can send messages. To do this each child in the class must have an email address.

COMMENTS

Please look at section 4, 'Web creation activities' (pages 85–100), or consult the book's website for tips and examples of student-generated web content.

2.5 Describing routines

LEVEL	**Beginner and above**
AGE	**8 and above**
TIME	**Part 1: 90 minutes; Part 2: 60 minutes**
AIMS	**To compare class routines in two different schools.** **Language:** Present simple tense.
PREPARATION	Explain the activity to the teacher at your partner school. Ask them to perform a similar task for your class to review.
MATERIALS	Worksheet 2.5, 'My daily routine'.

IN CLASS

Part 1

1 Ask the children to describe a typical school day. *When do you arrive at school? How do you get here?* (Drive, take school bus, walk ...?) *Do you stay in the same room or switch classes for activities? When is recess, lunch, etc.? When do you go home?*

2 Distribute the worksheet to the children. Assign small groups (or pairs) of children one particular day of the week.

3 Send the results desribing the daily routine to your partner school.

Part 2

1 Print out the routines sent from the partner school.

2 Have the children compare the routines. Where are the differences and similarities?

3 Ask the children which routine they prefer.

VARIATION	Children find out daily routines of the police, fire department, nurses, teachers, post office clerks, etc., and compare them with each other (for instance a nurse's day versus a firefighter's day).
FOLLOW-UP 1	For homework ask the children to go home and ask their parents about their daily routines.
FOLLOW-UP 2	Instead of a daily routine worksheet, distribute a weekly routine sheet, or even a monthly one, in this case, noting key events by the day, not by the hour.

2.6 Houses around the world

LEVEL

Elementary and above; you can adjust it to your particular group

AGE

8 and above

TIME

3 × 40 minutes minimum

AIMS

To learn about how people live in other countries; to describe and compare houses.

Language: Vocabulary of houses and homes; comparatives, simple adjectives.

MATERIALS

Scanner and/or digital camera.

PREPARATION

Familiarize yourself with an appropriate website—see step 2.

IN CLASS

Part 1

1 Explain to the children that people live in many different kinds of houses around the world. Ask them if they can name some houses they know from other countries: *teepees, igloos, floating houses, castles, farms,* etc.

2 Show the children some pictures of houses around the world. See 'Countries and cultures: houses' in section 7, page 114, for possible websites.

3 Ask the children which house they would like to live in and why.

4 Tell the children that you want them to find out about houses in different parts of the world.

5 Explain that they will do this by asking partners in a particular country for information about their houses and pictures to go with them.

6 Split the class into small groups and let them choose a country to investigate by drawing strips of paper out of a bag with the email address of a partner school.

7 Ask the children to write an email to the partner school explaining the project. Provide them with the copies of the template in this book.

8 Check the children's letter for mistakes and when it is ready, send it off.

Part 2

1 Ask the children to check their email for messages. In this activity, it might be a good idea to use a discussion group list (see the section on 'Working with e-groups and discussion lists', page 18), since all emails will be sent to the same address.

2 Let the children print out the answers if possible.

3 Ask the children to compare their houses to those of the partners. Ask them what is the same and what is different.

4 Have the children create a short presentation of their partners' houses. This can be either a paper poster or a PowerPoint slide presentation.

Part 3

1 Tell the children that it is now their turn to give their partners some information. Ask the children to take photos of their homes or draw pictures. Scan any art or non-digital photos.

2 Let each child write a short description of where they live. For beginners you can give them sentence stems to work from.

VARIATION

For children with advanced English skills leave out the communication aspect of the activity and assign the children a type of house to research on the Internet. The more exotic the house, the better.

FOLLOW-UP 1

Put information from both schools on a shared website. (See 'Web hosting: free services' in section 7, page 112.)

FOLLOW-UP 2

Broaden the project to include many different schools from around the world.

2.7 Pocket money

LEVEL

Elementary and above

AGE

8 and above

TIME

45 minutes (for preparing email); 45 minutes for reading and discussing email from the partner school.

AIMS

To compare and discuss pocket money rules.

Language: Numbers, chores, *How much...?, Do you...?, wh-*questions, present simple tense, comparatives, superlatives.

MATERIALS

Worksheet 2.7, 'Pocket money survey'.

IN CLASS

Part 1

1 Ask the children in your class if their parents give them money each week to spend. Tell them you want them to fill out a pocket money survey (worksheet 2.7) and give it to you when they are finished. (Note: this can be a sensitive issue. The children need not put their names on the surveys.)

2 Break the class up into small groups. Mix up the surveys and distribute an equal number to each group.

3 Ask each group to compare surveys and quantify the information. For example: *Three children get pocket money, two do not.* Or *All five children do chores.*

4 Add the group information together to create a class survey. Ask each group to fill in one or more of the survey questions, depending on the number of groups.

5 Attach the survey results to an email to your partner school or post them to you school website and send an email to your partners inviting them to log on. (See section 4, 'Web creation activities', pages 85–100.)

Part 2

1 Print out the surveys received from the partner school.

2 Ask the children to compare the results:
   – *What is the highest amount of pocket money?*
   – *How many people have to do chores?*
   – *What are the most popular items children buy with their pocket money?*

3 Ask the children to discuss the differences between the results of their survey and the partner school.

VARIATION	If you have created a Yahoo Group you can create a poll for all group members to fill out. Yahoo will generate the results of the poll. (See 'Search engines: general' in section 7, page 111, for the web address.)
FOLLOW-UP 1	Create an email discussion on the question: 'How much pocket money should children get?'. This can be done by simple email between two schools or by creating a discussion list. (See the section on 'Working with e-groups and discussion lists' on page 18.)
FOLLOW-UP 2	Host a global email project on pocket money and have your class maintain a website where partners can post their ideas and documents.
COMMENTS	This activity is best when done as a multi-partner project.

2.8 How do you know it's spring/summer/autumn/winter in X/Y/Z?

LEVEL	**Pre-intermediate; elementary for variation**
AGE	**10 and above**
TIME	**3 × 45 minutes**
AIMS	**To strengthen creative thinking skills and geographical awareness.**

Language: Vocabulary and phrases related to the seasons.

MATERIALS

Worksheet 2.8, 'What's the weather like around the world?'

IN CLASS

1 Introduce the subject by describing to the children something that tells you that a new season is approaching. This could be a change in temperature or store decoration, or leaves falling, or a harvest festival. It might also be something less obvious like the smell of burning wood or coal. You will probably have to do this in the children's mother tongue.

2 With the whole class, brainstorm some ideas and then divide up the class into small groups or pairs depending on the size of the class. Have them discuss all the seasons and come up with some ideas.

3 Circulate among the groups and provide language help where necessary. The children will certainly discuss things in their mother tongue but be sure the results are in the target language.

4 Come together as a full class. Have each group describe their ideas. Put them up on the blackboard. Sort them according to seasons. Point out any repetitions to the children.

5 Give out copies of the worksheet and then go online in groups of four. Give each group a season and get them to use the worksheet to record their ideas.

6 Ask each group to send the completed worksheets to their partner school via email.

7 When the partner schools respond compare ideas. See if your students can explain why the partners think the way they do.

VARIATION

1 Have your children and those of the partner school each create a web page describing a particular season in their home town. Provide children at the elementary level with sentence stems to work from. Let them post photographs or drawings to the page.

2 Send the web page as an attachment, or if you have a school website, post the page there and send an email to the partner school with the exact web address.

3 When you receive or can access your partner's presentation, print it out and ask the children to describe it.

4 Send the partner school an email acknowledging receipt of the web page. Thank them for it.

FOLLOW-UP 1

This activity is especially fun if you make it a multiple-partner project with contacts around the world. Collect all the information and/or web pages and create a poster display for your school about seasons around the world.

FOLLOW-UP 2

This activity also combines nicely with the web search activities 3.5 'Holidays around the world' and 3.8, 'How's the weather?'.

| COMMENTS | You may want to connect this activity to work in other subject areas such as basic geography, social studies, and science (weather). |

2.9 The 'Elympics'

| LEVEL | Elementary and above; you can adjust the language to suit the level of the group. |

| AGE | 8 and above |

| TIME | 40 minutes to set up the activity and then ongoing: depends on the nature of the competition—one-day event or recurring series. |

| AIMS | To compare the results of a competition.
Language: Comparatives, superlatives, simple past, numbers … |

| MATERIALS | Worksheet 2.9, 'The "Elympics"', for tracking results of the competitions, a stopwatch, measuring stick, or sports equipment (depends on the competitions chosen), and a digital camera to photograph the competition. |

| PREPARATION | Before introducing the activity, agree with the partner schools a time span within which they must submit their results. |

| IN CLASS | 1 Introduce the subject of the Olympic Games to your class. Ask them what kind of sports are played at the Olympics. Make a list of these sports. If you are combining this activity with the school 'field day', talk about which competitions are planned.
2 Hand out the 'Elympics' worksheet. Explain to the children that you are going to hold an 'Elympics' at school and that the partner schools are going to do the same.
3 Play the 'Elympics' events. If possible, take photos with a digital camera.
4 Record the results of the events on the worksheet and send the sheet and the photos to your partner schools.
5 As the partner schools send in their results, record them on a master worksheet. |

| VARIATION 1 | If you want to make this more elaborate, your class can be the organizers of the 'Elympics', organize an opening ceremony and awards ceremony, and declare the winners of each event. You may also want to design a uniform or gold, silver, and bronze medals to print out. |

| VARIATION 2 | The events needn't be traditional sporting events but can be 'wacky' and less physical in nature: for example, egg toss, how long you can keep a book on your head, or Tug of War. |

VARIATION 3

Note that this activity does not need to be physical in nature. Any measurable activity can be compared.

COMMENTS

The 'Elympics' is a particularly interesting cross-curricular option combining the Internet and physical education. It is a long-distance version of a school 'field day' with a variety of sports competitions. If your school has such a 'field day', it would be fun to integrate it into this activity.

2.10 A look in my fridge

LEVEL

Elementary and above; the currency converter may require more language.

AGE

8 and above

TIME

60 minutes online (if using a supermarket website)

AIMS

To compare food shopping customs in different countries.
Language: Numbers, food vocabulary, comparatives.

MATERIALS

Worksheet 2.10, 'Grocery list'.

IN CLASS

1 Ask the children if they ever go shopping for food. What do they typically buy? (If they don't shop themselves, they can ask their parents.) Distribute the worksheet and ask the class to make a shopping list.

2 Log on to a local supermarket website and search for prices. If there is no website of this kind, either take a field trip to a store or ask the children to find out the prices together with their parents. Attach the grocery list with prices to an email and send it to the partner school.

3 When the partner school sends their grocery list, go over the items with the class.
   - *What items are different?*
   - *Is there anything they don't know?*
   - *Is there anything not available in a local store?*

4 Ask the class to open a currency converter site on the Internet. (See activity 3.10, 'Currency converter'.) Explain how they work. Split the class up into small groups and ask them to convert the prices from the partner school into local currency.

5 Compare prices for items found on both lists. Why do they think some items may be more or less expensive?

VARIATION 1

Instead of shopping at a supermarket, have the children collect menus from restaurants—maybe even chains that share similar items. For instance, compare McDonalds in France to McDonalds in the USA. What are the items called? Are there some items on the menu in France that don't exist in the USA?

VARIATION 2

This activity can be conducted within the class itself, instead of with a partner school. The children search the supermarket websites and compare their respective shopping lists. In this case, the steps with the email and currency converter would be skipped.

COMMENTS

This is an example of a very practical type of communication activity called 'parallel structures'. In these activities, two or more partners or teams perform the same task and then compare and report their results to the whole class.

2.11 Cumulative story

LEVEL

Pre-intermediate and above; elementary, if you distribute a sentence stem list.

AGE

8 and above

TIME

60 minutes for basic version; ongoing for partner variation.

AIMS

To write a logical story or narrative.
Language: Depends on the context and the class guidelines.

PREPARATION

Create a handout with the email addresses of all the children in the class.

IN CLASS

1 Divide your class up into groups of 4–6 or put each pupil at a terminal if you have the equipment.
2 Tell the children that you want each group to start a story and send it to another group in the class. Start them off by writing the following sentence stem or something similar: *Once upon a time there was* .... Older and more advanced children can start something off on their own.
3 Explain to the children that they should send their story stem to another group in the class. Hand out a sheet with email addresses. The children should send their emails to the address directly below theirs on the list. If they are at the bottom, they move to the top of the list and work down.
4 Give the children 7–10 minutes to work out their installment. If working in groups, have one child dictate the words while another types the input into the computer. The remaining children should check for mistakes.
5 Send the emails. Each group should now receive a new story in their mailbox.
6 Give each group 7–10 minutes, as in step 4, to add to the story stem they received.
7 Continue as often as time allows or declare when a final round must end the story.

8 Ask the children to send you the finished stories. Print them out and give them to the children.

VARIATION 1

Create a cumulative story with a partner school. If you are well organized, you can even match specific groups from each class to create a number of stories and get more involvement than if it was a whole-class exchange.

VARIATION 2

Select a particularly interesting photograph (a dramatic landscape, a situation, even a work of art) and send it to all the children in your group. Now each child (or group) must start a story based on the same stimulus. Compare the final stories.

VARIATION 3

For elementary students you can create a list of sentence stems, which the children can refer to when writing their instalments.

FOLLOW-UP

Let each group create a slide show or a web page for their stories with photographs and/or illustrations. See section 4, 'Web creation activities', pages 85–100, for more ideas for this kind of activity.

COMMENTS

If your class is very confident, skip the in-class version and go straight to establishing an email project with another school.

2.12   Conducting an interview

LEVEL

Elementary and above

AGE

8 and above

TIME

Part 1: 60 minutes; Part 2: 90 minutes +

AIMS

To conduct an interview with an adult and learn about their profession.
Language: Open—depends on level, type of interviewee chosen, and needs of curriculum.

PREPARATION

Before introducing this activity, contact local citizens who work in a job that interests your children and who have Internet access and English skills. Remember that they needn't have access in the office if they can reply from home. If possible, select enough potential interviewees for each group of 4–6 children. If you cannot find any English speakers in your community, you may want to find a partner in an English-speaking country and have them organize interviews for your school.

IN CLASS

Part 1

1 Talk with the children about different jobs in their town. Introduce relevant vocabulary.

2 Tell the children that they will have a chance to ask some questions to the people they just talked about. Can they think of any questions to ask? Intermediate students can probably form many questions by themselves. Elementary students will require stems such as:

    –What time ... (What time do you go to work?)
    –When ... (When do you eat lunch?)
    – Do you ... (Do you catch criminals?)
    – How many ... (How many hours do you work?)
    – How much ... (How much holiday do you have?)

3 Give each group the email address of one worker. They must now write the questions in the email. Check for accuracy. Show the children how to introduce themselves politely to the interview partner.

4 Send the emails and tell the children they will check the responses the following week (to allow the workers to respond).

Part 2

1 Split the class into groups and have the children check their emails. If they don't know how to do it on their own, show them.

2 Let the children read the responses. Circulate and help them with any language they don't understand.

3 Each group now gets up and reports what they learned from the email.

4 Make sure the children write an email thanking the interview partner for their time.

FOLLOW-UP 1

Have the children create a web page on the profession they chose. They can illustrate their pages with images they find on the web. Better, if the person they interviewed is local, they can make digital photos of the person and their place of work, or they can ask them to send photos for scanning.

FOLLOW-UP 2

If it is not possible to create a web page, the children can create a 'Profession poster' or collage.

FOLLOW-UP 3

If the interviewees are local, organize a field trip and visit them.

FOLLOW-UP 4

Continue the email exchange and let the children ask more questions.

COMMENTS

Today, most public institutions such as the police, the fire department, the mayor's office, etc. have Internet access and an email address. What a great opportunity to prepare for a field trip, or for your children to learn about different professions without you having to organize one!

2.13   Riddles

LEVEL

Elementary and above

AGE

8 and above

TIME

60 minutes +

AIMS

To create riddles on topics learned in class and guess them.
Language: Depends on topic.

IN CLASS

1 Explain the concept of a riddle by doing a simple one with the class. For instance, if you are working on animals you could say: *It lives in Africa. It has black and white stripes. It looks like a horse.*

2 Tell the children that you want them to create riddles and send them to their classmates via email.

3 Depending on computer availability, give each child or group of children the email address of someone else in the class to send the riddle to.

4 Give the children time to come up with their riddle. Move about and help where necessary. When each child (or group) is ready, send the emails.

5 Each group should immediately receive their email. Tell them to open the email and try and solve the riddle. They should send their answer back via return email.

6 If the answer is wrong, the riddle makers must send another email with an additional hint. If they can't guess after three further hints, reveal the answers.

VARIATION 1

If you have a partner school, send the riddles to them and have them send your pupils riddles in return.

VARIATION 2

Combine images with written clues. For example: *It lives in ...* (picture of map of Africa). The children can search for images on the web engines or use clip art.

VARIATION 3

Let the children invent riddles and send them to you or to their parents.

COMMENTS

This activity is a good prelude to an online treasure hunt or web search. As in activity 2.11, 'Cumulative story', skip the in-class version if your class is confident, and go straight to Variation 1.

2.14   Word switch

LEVEL

Pre-intermediate (but can be modified)

AGE

8 and above

TIME

60 minutes for basic version

AIMS

To understand a text and recognize parts of speech; to work with a word-processing program.

Language: Depends on text.

MATERIALS

Strips of paper with children's email addresses.

PREPARATION

1 Prior to class, write a simple text in a word-processing program (approximately 5 lines) that is relevant to your class and that they should readily understand.

2 Go through the text and underline one word per sentence. If possible vary the type of word (noun, verb, adjective, etc.).

3 Attach the document to an email and send it to all the children in your class.

IN CLASS

1 Ask the children to open their email and the attached document. (Show them how to open attachments, if they haven't done it before.)

2 Tell them that you would like them to replace the underlined words with words of their own choice. Explain that the words can be silly but they must form grammatically correct sentences. They must use the cut and paste or highlighting features of their word-processing or email application to do so.

3 When complete ask the children to choose one of the strips of paper you prepared before class.

4 The children email their new text to the classmate on the strip of paper, who checks the email for grammaticality. They can also simply print out their texts and distribute them as hard copy. Monitor this step and provide help to the editors where necessary.

5 Let the children read their new 'silly' stories to the class.

6 Ask the children to email their finished stories to you. Compile them in one document and print a copy for each child.

VARIATION 1

Children at intermediate level and above can write their own short story, underline words, and email them to other students.

VARIATION 2

With older students, create a story and replace a content word with its grammatical category (noun, verb, adjective, adverb, article, etc.). The children must find a word from the appropriate category.

VARIATION 3   Have your entire class collaborate on a larger gap story that is then sent to a partner school, which sends the same to your class.

COMMENTS   In selecting underlined words, be sure that lower-level students have an adequate vocabulary base to replace them. Keep it simple: animals, family members, actions verbs, etc. Let them have fun and replace, for example, an animal with a family member.

3 Web search activities

One of the great criticisms of traditional coursebooks is their lack of authentic material. The Internet provides a solution. It is a treasure chest of information that can provide children with a first-hand glimpse into the lives and cultures of people around the world. But as much as this new information source teaches us about others, it also helps us reflect on ourselves This notion of learning about ourselves by looking at others is at the heart of many of the activities in this section.

Web searching is a complex task and requires children to make sophisticated logical decisions. They must draw parallels and look for relationships in a very undefined information space. In this way they strengthen both their critical and creative thinking skills and thereby support their learning across the curriculum.

The following activities represent a selection of web search activity 'genres' which can be applied to the teaching of a variety of topics. They are templates for teachers to use and modify according to need. Most of the activities also contain suggestions for web creation in the Variations and Follow-ups.

Links to websites are included, sometimes within the activities and always in section 7. Please check the website accompanying the book for downloadable templates, additional suggestions, and notification of any broken links.

3.1 The day I was born

LEVEL

Pre-intermediate and above

AGE

10 and above

TIME

90 minutes +

AIMS

To research facts about the day a child was born.
Language: Simple past.

PREPARATION

There are many websites that offer information on birthday facts. See 'Birthdays' in section 7, page 113, for some. Note that many are heavily Anglo-American in orientation and you may have to modify your search accordingly.

IN CLASS

1 Ask the children to tell you their birthdays. Tell them yours. (Boy, are you old!!!). State a fact about something that happened on your birthday. (*The first moon landing, the number one hit in the* US *charts was 'Purple Haze' by Jimmy Hendrix...*)

2 Tell the children that you are going to give them a list of websites where they can find information about what happened the day they were born.

3 Tell the children you want them to answer some questions about their birthday. Some successful questions are listed below, but you may want to add your own:

– *Find out what famous people were born on your birthday.*
– *What day of the week were you born?*
– *What was the weather like on the day you were born?*
– *Calculate how many minutes/days old you are.*
– *What was the top music hit/movie on the day you were born?*
– *Did anything important happen on the day you were born?*

4 Let the children search the sites you chose. Move about the room and help where necessary. If you have only a few terminals, you may have to break the project up over a series of days or assign the search as homework.

5 Once the children have completed their worksheets ask them to write a short story entitled *The Day I was Born* based on the information they collected. For lower-level students you may want to provide sentence stems.

FOLLOW-UP 1

You may want to initiate a web project with other schools. Register your project at one of the common web registry sites and collect information from your partners. Alternatively, you may want to search existing projects (there are many of this kind) and join them. (See 'Finding partners' in section 7, page 110.)

FOLLOW-UP 2

Take the stories and create a timeline to display in the classroom. You may want to solicit more birthdays from partners until you have an entire year of individual birthday stories.

FOLLOW-UP 3

If someone famous was born on your children's birthdays, let them investigate this person and tell the class about him or her.

3.2 The town tourist office

LEVEL	**Pre-intermediate and above**
AGE	**8 and above**
TIME	**Part 1: 60 minutes; Part 2: 90 minutes (45 minutes written work, 45 minutes web search and craft).**
AIMS	**To get tourist information about a town.**

Language: *There is/there are*, present simple tense, simple past tense, dates, numbers, *wh*-questions.

MATERIALS   Worksheet 3.2, 'My town'.

PREPARATION   Select a local municipal website with an English version. If the local town does not have such a site, choose the nearest larger town or city. You may also want to include a link to a travel site. (See 'Travel' in section 7, page 118, and the book's website, for options.)

IN CLASS

Part 1

1 Ask the children to imagine they are planning a trip to their town. What would they need or want to know? What questions would they ask? Distribute the worksheet and help them to understand the information they need to fill it in. Some questions you can ask are:

    –*Where is the town?*
    –*What is its population?*
    –*When was it founded?*
    – *How can you get there?*
    –*What is the weather like?*
    –*What are the major tourist attractions?*
    –*Where can you stay?*

    Let the children come up with more obscure questions as well.

2 Divide the children into small groups and ask them to log on to the websites you have selected. Explain that they must look for information to answer the questions they come up with. The information may be in the pupils' mother tongue, but keep the discussion in English. Help the class with terminology or ask them to use a dictionary

3 Compile the information and fill in a master copy of the worksheet with the entire class.

Part 2

1 With the information created in Part 1, ask the children to create a travel brochure for their town. Make sure they use full sentences when writing down the information. In large classes break into small groups and give each group a particular subject

to focus on such as: tourist attractions, transportation, food and restaurants, where to stay.

2 Allow the children to print out photos or other pictures from the web and use them to create a hard-copy brochure or poster presentation. They can use the worksheet as a template or create their own.

VARIATION 1   Instead of looking for 'Our town', look for 'Our country'. This makes finding information on the web in English easier. It also ensures that children from small villages can find relevant information in English.

VARIATION 2   Make an online brochure. See section 4, 'Web creation activities', pages 85–100, and the book's website for more details.

FOLLOW-UP 1   Exchange travel brochures with a partner school.

FOLLOW-UP 2   Present your travel brochure to the city tourist office.

3.3 Our twin

LEVEL   **Pre-intermediate and above**

AGE   **8 and above**

TIME   **90 minutes**

AIMS   **To compare information.**
Language: Comparatives, present simple tense, past simple tense, dates, geography vocabulary, numbers.

MATERIALS   Another copy of worksheet 3.2, 'My town', and an atlas for step 4.

IN CLASS
1 Go over the information on the chart created in the previous lesson.

2 Ask the children to search in different search engines to see if they can find towns with the same name.

3 If you cannot come up with any matches, try translating the name of the town into English and then searching (for instance: *Hirschberg—Deer Mountain*, or *Dos Rios—Two Rivers*).

4 If that doesn't work, tell them they can decide on a twin for their town. Elicit a country to choose from and show them a map. Let them select a city or town.

5 Once you have found towns that match, the children fill in the chart as in activity 3.2. Compare the results between the twin town and the home town.

6 Ask the children to find out how to get from their home town to the towns they selected.

3.4   Calendars around the world

LEVEL

Intermediate and above

AGE

10 and above

TIME

90 minutes + online

AIMS

To think about and compare different ways cultures express time.

Language: Comparatives, numbers, days, months, years, geography vocabulary.

MATERIALS

Worksheet 3.4, 'Calendars around the world'.

IN CLASS

1 Ask your class to tell you the days of the week and months of the year in English. Ask them how many days are in an English year. Do they have the same calendar in their native country? If not, what is different?

2 Tell the children that there are many different calendars in use around the world and many other calendars that were used in the past but have disappeared. They are going to work in groups and investigate different calendars and make a report for the class.

3 Break the class up into groups and put the names of calendars into a hat. Some good calendars to use are:
   – Julian Calendar
   – Islamic Calendar
   – Mayan Calendar
   – Chinese Calendar

4 Distribute to each group a set of web addresses (or perhaps just one) where they can find information about each calendar.

5 Distribute the worksheet. Have the children answer the following questions, filling in the worksheet as appropriate:
   – *How many days are there in a year?*
   – *Is the calendar based on the moon, the sun, or the earth?*
   – *What are the names of the days of the week?*
   – *What are the names of the months of the year?*
   – *How many months are there in the year?*
   – *Where do people follow this calendar?*

6 Have the children create a short presentation on their calendar. They can do this as a slide show or as a printed copy to display in their classroom. Let them search for images in a web browser. Remind them how they can cut and paste images to an electronic file.

FOLLOW-UP

An intriguing question to ask about calendars is whether they have a starting date. Many do. Ask the children to find out why the calendars begin when they do.

COMMENTS

1 This is quite a complex task and will probably require 'framing' in the mother tongue. However, the children can be required to report the results in the target language. In addition, it teaches cultural awareness and hopefully fosters tolerance and understanding of why things are done differently around the world.

2 Telling time is not the same around the world. Different cultures have varying approaches to recording what day it is, what month, etc. Looking at world calendars gives us a window into a different culture and generates lots and lots of language. See 'Time and date' in section 7, page 118, for some excellent websites.

3.5   Holidays around the world

LEVEL

Pre-intermediate

AGE

10 and above

TIME

60 minutes +

AIMS

To read and interpret a calendar.

Language: Days, months, years. Names of key holidays/festivals, present simple tense (or past depending on level), *wh*-questions (when corresponding with a partner).

IN CLASS

1 Explain to the children that just as we have different calendars, countries have different holidays, too. Some are religious, like Christmas, Ramadan, etc., while others are national, like Independence Day, etc.

2 Write the following web address on the board: *http://www.earthcalendar.net/*

3 Tell the children to go in groups to the computer and access this site. Show them how to navigate and let them experiment freely for a few minutes. Circulate between the groups to make sure they understand how the site works.

4 Now ask each group to select a country. Write the names of the countries up on the board.

5 While the children are still at the computers ask them questions:

– Are there any holidays in your country in March? in April? in June?

6 Have the children print out the yearly holiday calendars.

7 Bring the groups together and have them create a combined calendar for all the countries being investigated. Ask the children:

– Are there any countries that share the same holidays?
– Do some countries have different holidays on the same day?

8 Choose a holiday that particularly interests the children. Look for partners in a country that celebrates this holiday or festival. Have the children create a set of questions to send to their partners. (See section 7, 'Finding partners', page 110, and section 2, 'Communication activities', pages 36–53.)

VARIATION 1

Choose one holiday or festival that is shared in many countries, for instance, Easter. Compare how the holiday is celebrated in each place.

VARIATION 2

If you cannot find suitable partners, you can conduct a web search on your own and pre-select sites you feel your children will understand which describe these holidays.

COMMENTS

This activity builds on activity 3.4. Children can now select a country and find out about its holidays and perhaps research their origins and the customs associated with them. The very practical website recommended in step 2 allows you to search for holidays by many criteria such as date, country, and religion, all in one clear, easy place.

3.6 World travel

LEVEL

Intermediate and above

AGE

10 and above

TIME

90 minutes to set up activity and then ongoing.

AIMS

To read itineraries and timetables and find information about destinations.
Language: Depends on scope of the task.

MATERIALS

Worksheet 3.6, 'We'd like to go to …'.

PREPARATION

Before class, pre-select a travel website which includes hotel and flight booking. See 'Travel' in section 7, page 118.

IN CLASS

1 Explain to your class that each week (or month) they will go on a journey to a different city or country. Let the children choose where they want to go by popular vote, or hang up a map of the world on the wall and blindfold one child and play 'Pin the plane on the city'.

2 Once you have established a destination tell the children that there is a lot to think about when taking a trip. Write *travel* in the middle of the board and draw a circle round the word. Ask children to create a mind-map of possible things to consider.

3 Once the children have come up with some ideas, write the following topics on the board:

Transportation: How do you get there? Can you take a train, fly? How long will it take? How far away is it?

Where can you stay? What are the best hotels in town?

Weather? What are the average temperatures? What is the five-day forecast? What do you need to pack?

Typical food

What can you do or see?

4 Divide the children into groups and assign them one of the topics to investigate. Distribute the worksheet and a list of web addresses for them to look for the information.

5 Come together as a whole class and let each group report their findings.

VARIATION   Create a web page on the country in question. (See section 4, 'Web creation activities', pages 85–100.)

COMMENTS   This activity provides an excellent opportunity to integrate many of the Internet skills that children may have learned working on other related activities in this book. It is probably best done after you have completed activity 3.8, 'How's the weather' and activity 3.11, 'Distances'.

3.7 Welcome to the Children's World Congress!

LEVEL   **Pre-intermediate and above**

AGE   **10 and above**

TIME   **90 minutes +**

AIMS   **To compile basic information about a country. To retrieve, understand and relate travel information.**

Language: Dates and times, *wh*-questions, present simple tense, geographical terms.

MATERIALS   Slips of paper with countries written on them and a small bag to keep them in. An atlas or map of the world.

PREPARATION   Select a travel website and learn how to use it. See 'Travel' in section 7, page 118, for some examples.

IN CLASS   1 Split the class up into two groups. Tell the one group that they have been named delegates to the Children's World Congress. Explain that children from around the world will meet to talk about things important to them.

2 Tell the other children that they are travel agents who will help them get there. Pair one delegate with one travel agent. Tell them the congress will be held in … (your choice).

3 Ask each delegate to choose a country that they will represent by taking a strip of paper from your bag.

4 Ask the children to find which country they are from on a world map. Help them if they are completely lost.
  – Sort the countries out by continent. (This can be a movement activity.)
  – Put the countries in alphabetical order.

5 Have the delegates go online and look for information on the country they selected. Some questions could be:
  – *Can you find the flag of your country?*
  – *What is the national currency?*
  – *What is the capital city?*
  – *What is the official language?*

6 While the delegates are collecting information on their countries show the travel agents how to use the Internet travel site you have chosen.

7 Tell the delegates to go to their travel agents and arrange transportation and hotel accommodation at the conference site.

8 Print out the itinerary.

VARIATION 1

Use a currency converter to translate the cost of the trip into the delegates' local currency. See activity 3.10, 'Currency converter'.

VARIATION 2

Organize a real Children's World Congress as a collaborative project and invite children from around the world to participate and talk about issues important to them. Ask the children what they would talk about at such a congress. You can do this quite easily by creating a discussion group for this purpose. With the polling function, you can quantify members' opinions on questions the children choose to create.

3.8 How's the weather?

LEVEL

Elementary and above

AGE

8 and above

TIME

60 minutes; ongoing for Follow-up 3

AIMS

To describe and compare weather in various parts of the world.

Language: Weather vocabulary, days of the week, months of the year, numbers, simple past tense, present progressive tense, future with *going to*, countries and continents, clothes, *because*.

PREPARATION

Learn how to use a common weather website. See 'Natural world' in section 7, page 116, for some suggestions.

IN CLASS

1 If you haven't done so already, introduce children to basic weather vocabulary in English such as *rainy*, *sunny*, *windy*, *snow*, *cold*, *hot*, etc. Refer to the website of your choice for the exact language input required. If possible, co-ordinate with a science teacher to integrate the English web work with the core curriculum.

2 Tell the children you want them to take a trip to a foreign city. Ask them if they have ever visited a city in another country or whether they have a place they always wanted to travel to. Write down their choices.

3 Divide the class into small groups and assign each group one city to investigate. Tell them that before they pack they need to know what the weather will be like.

4 Ask the children to log on to the weather website you have chosen to use. Be sure it has clear navigation.

5 Demonstrate where to click for this information if necessary. Check to see if they are at the right place.

6 If possible, have the children print out the web page with the weather forecast for the chosen city. If this is not possible, create a chart which the children must fill in from the website.

7 Ask each group to decide on what they will pack for their trip and explain why.

8 In a whole class activity, ask the children to compare weather in the various cities. Which has the highest temperature? Where is it raining, snowing, etc.? This can be done by mixing groups or as a whole class activity.

VARIATION

Pair groups together and have the children ask each other about the weather in their chosen cities. Let the children formulate the questions on their own or offer some examples depending on language level, such as:

–*What is the temperature?*
–*Will it rain tomorrow?*
– *Did it snow yesterday?*

FOLLOW-UP 1

Make a bar graph of temperatures, amount of rain, etc. in your town, a partner city, or a random location of your choice.

FOLLOW-UP 2

Each group now role plays the weather report for the city they worked on. If possible video-tape the report.

FOLLOW-UP 3

Make this an ongoing project. Create a weather chart that the children can fill in each morning. If you have a partner school you can check the weather with them.

3.9 Common phrases

LEVEL	**Elementary and above**
AGE	**10 and above**
TIME	**90 minutes**
AIMS	**To identify common phrases one needs to know when travelling to a foreign country.**
	Language: Can be geared to language level and topics chosen.
MATERIALS	A foreign-language phrasebook.
PREPARATION	Select a translation website and learn how to use it.
IN CLASS	1 Ask the children if they have ever travelled to a foreign country where they did not speak the language.

2 Tell them that to make a journey easier, you often bring a phrasebook with you on your trips. If you have one, show it to the class and read a few passages from it. Write down a few headings from the Table of Contents:

   – *Simple greetings*
   – *Ordering at a restaurant*
   – *Travelling*
   – *Going to the movies*

3 Ask the children if they can think of any other things they would like to talk about in a foreign country. Add their suggestions to the headings above.

4 Take one of the headings and ask the children to come up with some common phrases they would need to know. For instance, if the heading was 'Restaurant', some of the phrases could be:

   – *Do you have. . .?*
   – *May I pay please?*
   – *I'd like . . . .*
   – *Waiter!*
   – *The food is cold!*

5 Break the children up into small groups. Assign each group a heading and have them try and write down five phrases they might need in this context. Circulate and check for accuracy.

6 Tell the children that you now need to find out what the phrases are in their mother tongue. They will do this by using the translation website you have chosen. Translation sites are often very literal and imprecise and this can yield quite hilarious results.

7 Demonstrate how the translation site functions.

8 Let the children type in their English phrases and record the results. Ask the children to make corrections if the translator gets their mother tongue wrong.

9 Translate the corrected mother-tongue phrase back into English and see if it yields the same phrase they came up with at the start.

VARIATION

Translate from English to a third language the children do not know. Let the children then create a three-way phrasebook for English, a third language, and their mother tongue. Find a native speaker of the third language to check the translations, or find a partner school from the country where the language is spoken, to co-operate with you.

COMMENT

This activity is good in conjunction with activity 3.6, 'World travel'. The Variation is fun and unusual since it puts the children in the position of 'native speakers' of English vis-à-vis a third language.

3.10 Currency converter

LEVEL

Pre-intermediate and above

AGE

8 and above

TIME

45 minutes + (depending on Follow-ups)

AIMS

To have children perform simple mathematical calculations and express relationships between facts.
Language: *How much, if . . . then*, simple past tense.

MATERIALS

Some local and foreign money, for example US dollars and Mexican pesos, or UK pounds and euros.

PREPARATION

Familiarize yourself with a good currency conversion site. See 'Countries and cultures: currency converter' in section 7, page 113 for an example.

IN CLASS

1 Show the children the local and foreign money you have brought to class. Write up on the board an equation which reflects the exchange rate, for example: *1 US$ = 3.5 pesos.*

2 Get the children to repeat the equation.

3 Split the class up into groups of 4–6 children per computer terminal. Ask them to type in the web address of the currency converter website you have chosen.

4 Take a moment to explain the website navigation. If you have a projector, perform a conversion for the whole group. Otherwise you may need to move from group to group or hand out screen shots to work from.

5 Tell the children it is their turn to make a conversion. Choose two fairly common currencies: yens to euros, etc. If you like, you can create a handout with the currencies on it for the children to choose from.

6 Ask the children what currencies they chose. Then say: *How much is ... in ...?*

FOLLOW-UP 1

Many currency conversion sites allow you to get past exchange rates as well as the current rate of exchange.

1 Ask the children what the exchange rate was: one week ago, two days ago, three months ago. You practise the past tense of the verb *be* and calendar language.

2 Have the children compare exchange rates:
On November 5 the dollar was lower/higher ....

3 Make this an ongoing project and record exchange rate fluctuations on a graph.

FOLLOW-UP 2

Make the activity interactive.

1 Send a partner school a list of items and ask them to quote prices for them in their local currency.

2 Convert the information into your local currency and compare prices.

3 Write back to your partner school and summarize the results:
Tell them:
Soap is more expensive in your country, but pens are cheaper.
You can also use phrases such as:
Soap is five cents more expensive than ....

COMMENTS

This is an all-purpose activity which can be used in many topic areas, such as shopping, travel, geography, and as part of other activities such as 2.6, 'Pocket money'.

3.11   Distances

LEVEL

Elementary and above

AGE

10 and above

TIME

90 minutes +

AIMS

To predict distances and work with different forms of measurement.

Language: *How far is it ...?*; *I think ....*; *How much is that in ...?*; simple mathematics and complex numbers.

MATERIALS

Worksheet 3.11, 'Distances'.

PREPARATION   Familiarize yourself with a website that calculates distances. See 'Countries and cultures: distances' in section 7, page 113, for examples.

IN CLASS

1 Show the children a map of a part of the world (for example, the USA). Tell them that the distance between New York and Miami is 1764 kilometres (or 1102 miles). Cite one or two other examples as well.

2 Hand out the worksheet to the children. Ask the children to guess the distance between the pairs of locations on the sheet. They should record their answers in the 'guess' column. Write down four of five distances from various parts of the world to help them estimate.

3 When they are finished, ask the class to tell you some of their predictions: *How far is it from London to Rome?*, for example. Record some of the results on the board.

4 Tell the class that they are now going to go to a website that calculates distances. Split the class into small groups. Give each group four routes to calculate. Give them the address (URL) of your chosen website.

5 Each group searches for the distances between their assigned points and puts them in the column next to their predictions.

6 Bring the class back together and ask each group to read off the actual distances between points. The other groups enter these distances on to their sheets.

7 Each child must now calculate the difference between their prediction and the actual distance. (They may need calculators for this.)

8 Go over each distance and see which child came closest to predicting it.

FOLLOW-UP 1   Once the distances have been established, ask the children to go to a distance conversion website you have familiarized yourself with. Ask the children to convert their results into different measurements. If they work with kilometres, ask for the distance in miles. Then ask them to calculate the distance in yards, centimetres, feet, or whatever else you may choose. This will certainly yield very large numbers. See if they can say these numbers.

FOLLOW-UP 2   Ask the children to guess how long it will take to get from point to point by different means such as car, bicycle, ship, aeroplane, and so on.

FOLLOW-UP 3   Once you have completed this activity, you can add it on to other activities such as 3.6, 'World travel', or 3.7, 'Welcome to the Children's World Congress!'.

COMMENTS This activity can be nicely integrated with geography, social studies, and mathematics classes.

3.12 Riding the metro

LEVEL **Pre-intermediate and above**

AGE **10 and above**

TIME **60 minutes**

AIMS **To read a map or timetable, and give directions.**

Language: Numbers, time phrases, present simple tense, questions, sequencing words.

PREPARATION Many countries have extensive rapid transit systems. On the web you can find sites with information on many of them, including maps and schedules. You will find some good links under 'Transportation' in section 7, page 118. Prepare a handout of links and familiarize yourself with a website of your choosing.

MATERIALS Handout of transportation websites. Worksheet 3.12, 'Metro'.

IN CLASS 1 Ask the children if they are old enough to drive a car. They should (hopefully) all say no.

2 Ask them how they can get from one place to another (from school to the shop, or from home to the swimming pool) if nobody with a car drives them. There will be many different answers depending on where the children live: bus, bicycle, tram, boat, perhaps even an aeroplane in remote regions.

3 Explain that in many big cities people take trains to work. Explain that these city trains have many names. Give them some examples: Subway (New York), Underground or Tube (London), Metro (Paris and Washington D.C.), BART (San Francisco).

4 Distribute the handout of city rapid transit system websites. In small groups or individually let the children choose a transit system to investigate. If you have limited computer times, download the subway maps to a local disk or simply print them out.

5 Have the children complete the worksheet. The sheet includes questions such as:

– *How many lines does the system have?*
– *What colours are the lines?*
– *Do the lines connect at a central station?*
– *Which line has the most stations?*

You may want to modify the questions according to the system chosen.

6 Many subway sites also give information on riding times. Ask the children to find out the riding time from the two stations located farthest apart. Get them to record their findings on the worksheet.

7 Still in groups (or pairs), the children ask each other how to get from one station to another. Get them to record their findings on the worksheet.

8 Move among the children and monitor their replies.

VARIATION 1 Make overhead transparencies or use a computer projector to display rapid transit maps from various cities. Choose children and ask them to explain how to get from one point to another. Focus on sequencing words such as: *first, then, after that…*

VARIATION 2 Work with a partner school. How do children get to school there? If they take public transport, ask the partners more about their local transport systems with questions similar to the ones on the worksheet.

3.13 What's the time, Mr Computer?

LEVEL **Elementary and above**

AGE **10 and above**

TIME **60 minutes +**

AIMS **Telling the time, simple mathematics.**
Language: *If … then …*; *I think it is …*; *What is the time difference?*; *ahead*; *behind.*

MATERIALS A teaching clock.

IN CLASS
1 Log on to an international time site. See 'Time and date' in section 7, page 118, for some examples.

2 Go to the full world clock page and call out a city. The first group to tell you the day and time wins. Repeat with seven or eight different locations. Write the locations up on the board.

3 Take two examples from the cities written on the board (for instance, New York and London). Say to the children: *It is 8 p.m. in London and it is 3 p.m. in New York. So the time difference is 5 hours.* Demonstrate with a clock.

4 Using the example cities listed on the board ask the children *What is the time difference between Abu Dhabi and Teheran?* Each group tries to work it out and calls out the answer.

5 Introduce the concept of ahead and behind. You may want to demonstrate the terms by lining up the children and explaining in terms of position.

6 Ask the children *Is Washington ahead of or behind Los Angeles?* Follow up with: *How far behind?*

7 Repeat one of the examples: *In Washington it is 3 p.m. and in London it is 8 p.m.* Add: *So, if it is 5 p.m. in Washington, it is 10 p.m. in London. If it is 6 p.m. in Washington, what time is it London?* Let the students answer.

8 Let the children go back to the website and choose some other cities. Have one group quiz the other and check that the answers are correct. Let them ask any of the above questions.

VARIATION

Let each group use a different date and time website.

COMMENTS

1 This is a simple, quick activity to get children familiar with sending requests to a computer, which practises using time phrases in English.

2 Most of the websites also include information on sunrise and sunset, moon phases, etc.

3.14   Department stores

LEVEL

Pre-intermediate and above; can be simplified

AGE

10 and above

TIME

Part 1: 60 minutes, Part 2: 60 minutes

AIMS

To scan a website for information; to decide on a gift and explain the decision.

Language: Time phrases, monetary amounts, descriptions, describing location, polite phrases.

MATERIALS

Worksheet 3.14, 'Department stores'.

PREPARATION

Major department stores in the US, UK and other English-speaking countries have extensive websites where you can do online shopping. Some sites are easier to navigate than others. Choose sites that are without clutter and have a clear structure. Some of these sites actually have floor plans of the store itself. Type *department store* in your web browser to get exact links, or see 'Shopping' in section 7, page 117, for some good examples. Familiarize yourself with some of your choosing.

IN CLASS

Part 1

1 Give the children the web addresses for department store websites. Let them click about on their own for a few minutes.

2 Hand them the department store worksheet. Tell them they must find certain features of each store and note them on the list. Some easy questions for the list are:

—What is the name of the store?
—Where is it located?
—What are the opening hours?
— How many departments has the store got?
—What are they?
—Where can you find the following items?
   a girl's dress/perfume/a basketball/a computer/a suit

3 Ask the children to note five new words they don't understand. They should send these words to the entire class via email to see if they can get an explanation from one of the other children (even in the mother tongue), or go to a translation website.

Part 2

1 In this session one group of children will be online with the web page of a department store open. A second group will act as customers.

2 Tell the children at the computer screen that they are the Help Desk of the store in question. They must answer the customers' questions. Give the customers a few minutes to come up with questions for the Help Desk. Questions could be (depending on level and content previously taught):

—Where is the shoe department?
— Do you have a restaurant?
— I'm looking for the toys.
—When do you close today?
— Have you got a lift?

3 The children who are the Help Desk refer to the website to find answers to the questions.

4 Encourage the children to role-play. Have the Help Desk use polite phrases such as: *May I help you? This way please. Of course.* The customers should respond in the same way, thanking the Help Desk for assistance.

VARIATION 1

Have each group choose a different department store. Let them compare prices for various items. Find the most expensive item and the cheapest.

VARIATION 2

Part 2 can be conducted offline as well, based on the information on the department store worksheet.

VARIATION 3

Have the children design their own floor plan for a store, using the department store website as a model. Use the children's store for part 2.

3.15 My local habitat

LEVEL

Elementary and above

AGE

8 and above

TIME

Part 1: 40 minutes; Part 2: 40 minutes

AIMS

To talk about animals and where they live.
Language: Animals, geography, *wh*-questions, present simple tense.

PREPARATION

Create a printout of the web page *http://www.enchantedlearning. com/biomes/*. You will probably need to pre-teach some vocabulary.

IN CLASS

Part 1

1 Ask the children in your class if they know where in the world elephants live. Ask them if they know where a polar bear lives. You may want to hold up flashcards of the animals.

2 Review the answers the children gave: *So an elephant lives in Africa or Asia*. Ask the children if they can name any other animals that live in Africa. Elicit animals such as giraffes or lions.

3 Explain to the children that some animals live in hot weather places, while others live in cold weather ones. Some like to live in wet places where it rains all the time, while others like it very dry. The place where an animal lives is called its *habitat*.

4 Distribute the printout of the web page.

5 Go over the various habitats with the children. Let them talk about what they know about habitats. It is all right if they use their mother tongue. Remodel and write the keywords in English on the board.

6 Split the class up into small groups. Assign each group a habitat to research. Tell them to go back to the website above and look for answers to the following questions:

– *What is the climate like in this habitat?*
– *Where in the world can you find such habitats?*
– *What animals live in these habitats?*

Part 2

1 Ask the class what habitat their home town belongs to.

2 In small groups ask the children to do the following:

– *Describe the location of their home town in the world. For example:* 'It is in the Northern hemisphere, on the continent of Asia, with Myanmar in the North and Malaysia in the south.'

You can also ask for latitude and longitude if the children are familiar with these concepts.

– Describe the climate in your home town.
– Describe animals that live in your home town.
– Describe plants that live in your home town. What kind of food can farmers grow?

3 Collect the descriptions from each group and put them in an email to a partner school. If you like, you can include photographs characteristic of the local landscape.

4 When the partner school responds with their own habitat email, compare the two habitats. List similarities and differences in two columns. See if any animals live in both places.

VARIATION Focus on endangered species. Introduce the animals and where they live, and explain why they are threatened. This is a project that can easily be combined with mainstream science activities.

3.16 Rivers

LEVEL **Pre-intermediate and above (depending on task)**

AGE **8 and above**

TIME **90 minutes +**

AIMS **Cross-curricular work on geography.**

Language: Comparatives, the vocabulary of geography and animals, *wh*-questions, present simple tense, simple past tense (depends on difficulty of task).

MATERIALS Handout of websites with information about rivers. (See 'Natural world' in section 7, page 116, for a starting point.) Worksheet 3.16, 'Rivers'. A map of the world.

PREPARATION Familiarize yourself with a website for each river you choose to discuss.

IN CLASS 1 Show the children a map of the world. Point to a large river near their home. Ask the children if they have heard of any other rivers.

2 Put a number of river names on pieces of paper. You may like to choose from this list of some of the longer rivers in the world: the Nile, the Mississippi, the Rhine, the Yangtze, the Amazon, the Mekong.

3 Split the class into groups of four and have each group select a piece of paper from a bag. This is the river they will investigate.

4 Hand out a list of websites about the chosen rivers. Tell the children they must find certain key information about the river. Hand out copies of the worksheet for them to fill in.

5 Give the children some free surfing time to learn anything else they want to know about the river. Encourage them to use the space on the worksheet headed 'Other interesting things about the river'.

6 Have the children ask each other questions about their rivers.

FOLLOW-UP 1

Each group of children creates a web presentation on their river. As an offline alternative, the children can create a slide presentation. If this is not possible either, let them make posters to hang up in the classroom.

FOLLOW-UP 2

Instead of focusing on the river itself, place the emphasis on 'life on the river' and work with the children to learn about cultures in the region. You might even want to contact a school in a town on the river. This is a project that could be combined with a social studies project.

COMMENTS

Geography is one of the most accessible topics for web exploration by young learners. Geography is very concrete and it can be easily visualized. Geography tasks are also quite flexible, allowing for work at varying language levels. The cross-cultural options are huge—from map drawing and science experiments to studies of local culture.

3.17 Volcanoes

LEVEL

Pre-intermediate and above

AGE

8 and above

TIME

60 minutes online (without the poster-making)

AIMS

To look at geographical locations and natural features.
Language: Prepositions, comparatives, superlatives, past tense.

MATERIALS

A4-size coloured card, glue. Worksheet 3.17, 'Volcanoes'.

PREPARATION

Hang a large map of the world on the wall (or simply draw the outlines of the continents).

IN CLASS

1 Show the children a picture of a volcano. Ask them if they have ever seen a volcano in real life. Teach some keywords such as *eruption*, *lava*, *cone*, etc.

2 Distribute a list of potential volcano-oriented websites. See 'Natural world' in section 7, page 116.

3 Tell the children that you want them to find as many volcanoes as possible and locate them on the big world map and put a pin at their location. Explain to the children that they must try and find out information about their favourite volcano. Distribute copies of the worksheet.

4 Ask the children to print out a photograph of their favourite volcano. Ask the children to arrange the volcanoes in order of size. If two children choose the same volcano they may work together or one child must choose another volcano.

5 Pass out A4 sheets of coloured card to the pupils. Glue each volcano photo on to a sheet of paper. Underneath the photos the children can add the information in the questions or glue their completed questionnaires to the card. Hang up the volcano sheets around the classroom.

VARIATION 1

Make a volcano web page or electronic slide presentation.

VARIATION 2

Instead of individual mini-posters, create a large class volcano poster.

FOLLOW-UP

The children can create an online document or poster to show the inside of a volcano and how it erupts.

COMMENTS

Volcanoes are exciting for children, but they directly affect many areas of the world, sometimes with catastrophic results. Be aware of this potential before introducing an activity focusing on a potentially destructive natural object or event.

3.18 Museum quest

LEVEL

Pre-intermediate and above

AGE

10 and above

TIME

Part 1: 45 minutes; Part 2: 45 minutes +

AIMS

Reading, describing objects of art, and explaining location.
Language: Descriptive adjectives, present simple tense, simple past tense, imperatives.

MATERIALS

Worksheet 3.18, 'At the museum'.

PREPARATION

Choose one museum website per small group. See 'Museums' in section 7, page 116, for some key websites. Review the sites and choose one art exhibit from each for the children to find.

IN CLASS	**Part 1**

1 Divide the class up into groups of 4–6 children.

2 Assign a museum address to each group of children in your class.

3 Explain to each group that they must find a specific work of art in the online collection. Give them hints on where to find them.

4 Once the children have found the piece, have them bookmark it. If they finish quickly let them browse the museum site at leisure. Once all the works have been found, the children must describe the objects using information from the website. They may choose to print out a picture of the object or the entire web page. Distribute copies of the worksheet and get them to fill in answers to the questions.

Part 2

1 Students return to their groups and write down instructions on how to find the art object on the website. Make sure the children are precise and use web terminology.

2 Groups exchange their directions and see if by following them they can find the objects.

FOLLOW-UP 1

This activity is very suitable for cross-curricular work. Consult with other subject-area teachers when making your choice of works of art.

– The children can relate the works of art to specific periods of history.
– They can locate the artist's place of residence on a map.
– They can identify the objects as examples of a school of art.

FOLLOW-UP 2

The class can create a gallery of their own with their favourite works of art from museums around the world. A note of caution: be sure to check on copyright laws if you are posting to your school's public website. (See the note on copyright on page 21.)

3.19   My favourite picture

LEVEL

Pre-intermediate and above; can be adapted to different levels.

AGE

10 and above

TIME

45 minutes online

AIMS

To describe works of art.

Language: Colours, feelings, shapes and any other descriptive vocabulary the children may have learnt.

MATERIALS

Worksheet 3.19, 'My favourite picture'.

PREPARATION   Pre-select museum or gallery websites, preferably in English-speaking countries. As seen in activity 3.18, 'Museum quest', the Metropolitan Museum of Art in New York has a great site with the entire collection online, as does the British Museum in London. See 'Museums' in section 7, page 116, for their website addresses. If you want more control, select a series of paintings with web addresses that the children must choose from.

IN CLASS   1 Explain to the children that you want them to choose a picture and describe it. Tell them to log on to the website and allow them 15 minutes to make their choice.

2 Have the children print out their pictures.

3 Distribute copies of the worksheet. Each pupil answers the questions about their pictures.

4 Ask a child to describe their picture to the rest of the class.

5 Pair off the children and let them compare their paintings.

FOLLOW-UP   This activity would work well as part of the larger project of a class museum. Each child can select a favourite picture to contribute to the class gallery.

COMMENTS   1 This activity is a logical follow-up to activity 3.18, 'Museum quest'. Children will already be familiar with museum websites that will make this task, which is simply a different perspective on art, easier to understand.

2 The Metropolitan Museum website has a feature to create a personalized collection called 'My Met'. You can make selections with the entire class or let each child create their own 'Met'.

3.20   Space facts

LEVEL   **Elementary and above**

AGE   **8 and above**

TIME   **45 minutes for initial lesson (steps 1–6). Website creation will be a project over many lessons, perhaps integrated into other classes across the curriculum (science and art).**

AIMS   **To learn some basic facts about our solar system and create a website displaying them.**

Language: Space vocabulary, numbers, prepositions, present simple tense, question words, descriptive adjectives.

MATERIALS   Worksheet 3.20, 'Planet facts'.

PREPARATION

You may want to create a homepage template for the space website for your children to link to and use as a design model.

IN CLASS

1 Show the children a diagram of the solar system. Write *Solar System* on the board.

2 Ask the children if they know the English names for the planets. In many languages they will be very similar to English.

3 Depending on the size of your class, split the class up into groups of 2–5 children.

4 Put the names of the planets in a bag and ask one child from each group to choose a planet.

5 Hand out the planet facts worksheet. Write three or four web addresses on the board and ask the children to search for answers to their questions on these sites. See 'Space' in section 7, page 117, for some good places to look.

6 Circulate from group to group and ask them to tell you some facts about their planets.

7 Create a Solar System website. Let each group create a page on their planet and link it to a website homepage. They can download pictures from the web or draw their own. If a web-based presentation is not possible, have the children make a PowerPoint or pen-and-paper presentation.

FOLLOW-UP1

Find out how the planets got their names. See 'Greek myths' in section 7, page 115.

3.21   The view from here

LEVEL

Elementary

AGE

8 and above

TIME

45 minutes

AIMS

To compare pictures and predict what they show.
Language: *I think,* the prepositions *of* and *from.*

IN CLASS

1 Ask the children to log on to the NASA Solar System Simulator. You will find the web address under 'Space' in section 7, page 117.

2 Explain to the children that normally, when we look at the planets, we see them from Earth. Explain that the Simulator will allow them to look at their chosen planets from many different positions.

3 Demonstrate the basic functions of the Simulator. If you have a projector you can do so for the entire class. Otherwise you may want to hand out screenshots to each group.

4 Ask each group to choose a view of their planet from another planet in the solar system, and print each of these views out.

5 Ask the children to place their views next to each other and compare them.

6 Allow the children to circulate and try and guess what the view is, using sentences like: *I think this is a view of Saturn from Mars.*

7 See if the children can recognize which picture is a view from their planet.

FOLLOW-UP

The Space Simulator also has views from a number of space probes travelling our solar system. From here the children can learn more about these missions. The NASA website has direct links to these projects, most of which have child-friendly pages on their websites. The children can track the progress of the missions, using their language skills to:

– describe the goals of the mission (present simple tense)
– its current status (present progressive tense—*The probe is passing Venus.*)
– its future course.

3.22 Me in space

LEVEL

Elementary and above

AGE

8 and above

TIME

45 minutes

AIMS

To compare conditions on different planets.

Language: Comparatives, superlatives, *much/many*, question words, present simple tense, numbers

PREPARATION

Consult with your science teacher colleague to see if the children have studied space already. If not, try and align this activity to their science lessons so that they have been introduced to concepts such as gravity before doing this activity.

IN CLASS

1 Tell the children that many things on earth are different on other planets. Ask them if they can think of any things they may know: for example, gravity, temperature, atmosphere.

2 Ask the children if they think a year on Mars is the same length as a year on earth. In small groups ask them to log on to the Exploratorium website to find out. You will find the web address under 'Space' in section 7, page 117.

3 Let each child type in their birthday and make a printout of the result.

4 Ask each group some random questions such as:

– *How old is Tommy on Jupiter?*
– *Is Johnny older or younger on Venus than on Pluto?*

5 Write down the question stems you want to use up on the board or as a handout.

6 Put two groups together and have them ask each other questions.

7 Get the attention of the entire class. Tell the students that not only is your age different on other planets, but also your weight. See if anybody can explain why. (Hint: gravity.)

8 Ask the children to log on to the Exploratorium website again and check their weight on other planets.

9 Follow the procedure as in steps 3–6.

3.23 Movies

LEVEL

Pre-intermediate and above

AGE

10 and above

TIME

60 minutes online

AIMS

To understand a schedule and describe a plot.

Language: Present progressive and present simple tenses, *wh-* questions, time phrases.

MATERIALS

Slips of papers with cities and theatres on them, in a bag. Worksheet 3.23, 'Movies'.

PREPARATION

Before class, identify a local or national movie directory. Good examples of national ones are listed under 'Entertainment: movies' in section 7, page 114. Prepare a class handout with a list of potential web addresses. If possible, choose sites from a variety of English-speaking countries such as the USA, Canada, UK, Ireland, New Zealand, and Australia.

IN CLASS

1 Ask your class if they have seen any movies lately.

–*What movies have you seen recently?*
–*Where did you see the movie?*

2 Tell the children that you want them to check and see what movies are playing in English-speaking countries. Tell them that they can find this information at websites you will be distributing.

3 Divide the class up into small groups.

4 One child per group chooses a slip of paper. Each slip of paper has the name of a city and a web address written on it.

5 Hand out the worksheets and get them to answer questions such as:

–What is the address of the cinema?
– How many movies are there at the cinema?
–When is the movie showing?
– How long is the movie?
–Who are the main actors?
–What is it about?

6 Bring all the groups together and compare their worksheets. Are the same movies showing? Do they have similar starting times? The children may want to compare the English sites to a local cinema schedule.

VARIATION 1 Instead of searching by city/cinema, search according to movie. In this case you can work with the term: *Where is ... playing?* and *Is it playing at ... ?*

VARIATION 2 Instead of looking for a movie cinema, the children can go to an Internet movie database and get information on the movie only.

FOLLOW-UP 1 Most major Hollywood movies now have their own websites. Let the children access the website of their favourite movie (or one of your choosing) and search the site independently. Often such sites come with clips and games. (For more information on using movies, see the book *Film* in this series.)

FOLLOW-UP 2 Go to a common translation site and ask the children to type in the English name of a movie and translate it into their native language, if the translator supports the language. Another option is to translate the title in the children's mother tongue back into English. The results are often really funny. Ask them how they would translate the titles. (See activity 3.9 for more on this.)

3.24 Premier league

LEVEL **Elementary and above, depending on task**

AGE **8 and above**

TIME **90 minutes or ongoing**

AIMS **To extract information from a table, to compare and work with simple statistics.**

Language: Present simple and present progressive tenses, simple past tense, *wh*-questions.

MATERIALS Worksheet 3.24, 'My favourite team'. If Variation 1 is chosen, a map of the UK or the country in question.

IN CLASS

1 Ask the children if they can name any football (soccer) teams outside their home country. Ask them to go to a map and show the class where they are located.

2 Tell them that they are going to find out information about British football. Have them go to the website of the premier league. You will find the web address under 'Sports' in section 7, page 117.

3 Quickly go over the architecture of the site with the children. Help them with any vocabulary they may not know.

4 Put the names of football teams in a hat. Have the children draw a team to investigate. Hand out the worksheet for them to fill out about the team of their choice.

5 Pair the children and have them ask each other questions from the questionnaire.

VARIATION 1

Use the website of UEFA or FIFA. In this case the children can investigate the country of any team they choose, including their own country.

VARIATION 2

This can be an ongoing project for the real fans among the children following their team of choice and reporting on its progress. The class can also make a table with pins for each team and move them up and down according to weekly results.

VARIATION 3

Instead of soccer choose another sport. Popular choices might be the NBA (basketball) or the NFL (American football). Their websites are listed under 'Sports' in section 7, page 117.

FOLLOW-UP

Group the pupils according to their favourite teams. Together they can create an unofficial team fan site. (See section 4, 'Web creation activities' pages 85–100.)

COMMENTS

Sports are full of statistics. Football was chosen here because of its universal appeal, but the activity is really applicable to any organized sport—cricket, baseball, ice hockey—it depends on the interests of the children. Be aware that this activity is time-sensitive as not all sports are played all year round.

3.25   Superstars

LEVEL   **Elementary and above**

AGE   **8 and above**

TIME   **40 minutes for search, variable time for presentations.**

AIMS   **To describe a favourite celebrity.**
Language: Language of description (can be adjusted to the language level).

MATERIALS   Large sheets of card, photograph of a celebrity, colour printer, coloured pens and markers, glue (depending on the end-product you choose).

IN CLASS

1 Show the class a photograph of a celebrity they will recognize. Tell the children that you are a fan and that you like this person very much.

2 Ask the children if they have a particular person they are a fan of. Who is their superstar? Write their choices on the board.

3 Tell the children that you want them to log on to the Internet and look for information about their superstar. Explain that they can look at sites in their mother tongue, but that they will make a poster about their superstar in English. Be sure that the children are searching in a childproof search engine (see section 7, 'Search engines: children-specific', page 111, for suggestions). Let the children print out pages with pictures or photos they want to use for their poster.

4 Depending on the language level of the children, you can ask them to make an independent search or answer a series of questions that you set out. These can include:
  –*What is your superstar's name?*
  –*What is your superstar's birthday?*
  – *Is your superstar a musician, actor, athlete, etc.?*
  –*Why do you like your superstar?*
  –*Why do you like your superstar?*

5 Once the children have completed their web search, distribute cardboard sheets and let them create their superstar posters. Before the children write on the posters directly, have them write their texts on a separate sheet. Check these sheets for correctness.

6 Display the posters in your school.

VARIATION 1   Rather than making a poster, let the children create a web page about their superstar (see section 4, 'Web creation activities', pages 85–100). You can link these individual pages to a class homepage.

VARIATION 2

Exchange superstar web pages with a partner school. If you don't feel comfortable creating web pages, scan the children's artwork and send it as an email attachment. If you exchange superstars, try and make them local celebrities. Encourage your class to ask the partner class questions about their superstar once they receive their email.

VARIATION 3

In large classes, you may want to limit the number of superstars and have children work in groups searching for information and making posters. In this case, elicit names of superstars and then let children choose one out of a hat, or group children according to their favourite star.

COMMENTS

This activity involves searching for information in the children's mother tongue.

4 Web creation activities

Contrary to what you might expect, web creation activities are probably initially easier for the foreign language learner (and teacher) to work with than web searches. Once you and the children have learned the basics of web design, you can determine content and match the task to the language and developmental level of your children—something which is harder to do when working on existing websites not geared to language learners.

Don't be afraid

When you look at a good website you might think only an expert can create something so sleek and of such high quality. But in fact, it is the ease with which one can create professional looking content that makes the web such an exciting tool for educators.

Don't be afraid of HTML code. It may look complex when you first see it, but it isn't very tricky. HTML merely gives your content (pictures, text, audio, etc.) a 'tag' which tells your web browser where the content should appear on the page. You really don't even need to understand it to create your web pages. Web editors, which work pretty much like a word-processing program, automatically translate your work into HTML code. So, what you see as you work on your document is what you get when it is displayed in your web browser. Of course it can't hurt to understand the basics, but you can do a lot without ever learning a single element of HTML code.

A good trick

Every web page displayed in your browser has a 'source code', the HTML information that your browser uses to build the page, built into the document. If you click on 'View' then 'Source', in Internet Explorer, for example, you will see the exact HTML programming for the page. If you like what you see, copy the code and simply replace the old content with your new information. In a flash, you have a new web page.

Practise offline

Don't forget that you can create a web page without having to go online. You can save a web page you create directly to your computer's hard disc or to another disc and later upload it to a host site on the web if you so desire. The outcome will look exactly the same online or offline. The only difference is the potential audience.

There are numerous free tools and tutorials for creating websites that are available on the Internet. We have listed some of the best links in section 7 under 'Creating websites', page 108, and on the book's website. In this section, our focus is less on the specific computer skills needed to create web pages than on their application. In other words, we want to give you some ideas on how you can apply your skills to benefit the language classroom.

4.1   What's it about?

LEVEL	**Elementary and above**
AGE	**8 and above**
TIME	**90 minutes +**
AIMS	**To introduce children to thinking about multimedia.** **Language:** Depends on children's input; basic web technological terminology.
PREPARATION	Be sure to have read the introduction to this section. You need to have acquired the basic skills needed to create a website before embarking on these activities with your children.
IN CLASS	1 Tell your class that you want to teach them how to make their own websites. Tell them that a website can be about anything they want.

1 Tell your class that you want to teach them how to make their own websites. Tell them that a website can be about anything they want.

2 Show them a few examples of random websites created by children and adults. Ask the children if they can guess what they are about.

3 Ask the children what subjects they can think of for a website. Write their ideas on the board.

4 Tell the children that you love the circus and you want to make a website about circuses.

5 Write the word *circus* up on the board and draw a circle around it. Tell the children that on your website you are going to describe a visit you had to the circus when you were a child. (Draw a line out from the circle to the word *story*.) Then tell the children that you also want to show photos of circuses. (Draw another arrow out to the word *photos*.) Finally, tell the children that you would like to get information about different circuses around the world by reading their websites. (Draw another line to the word *links*.) *That's my website*, you can tell them.

6 Split the class up into small groups or pairs. Ask them to select a subject for their website from the options on the board and create a mind map following your example.

7 Circulate and provide input. Be sure the children keep it simple and realistic.

COMMENTS	For children with only a beginning knowledge of computers, limit the options to text and pictures. For older children with advanced computer skills, you can allow them to introduce video, audio, and animation.

4.2 'Design it' dictation

LEVEL	**Elementary and above**
AGE	**8 and above**
TIME	**60 minutes**
AIMS	**To describe and understand the location of objects on a web page; to design a clear web page.** **Language:** Prepositions, web terminology.
MATERIALS	Some large pieces of paper, at least one for each child.
IN CLASS	1 Once the children have created a mind map of their website's content (see activity 3.1, 'What's it about?'), they need to think about where the content should be placed on the various pages. Tell them you want to design their homepage first.

2 Show the children some examples of websites created professionally and by children. (See the book's website for sites listing class web pages.)

3 Introduce some vocabulary to do with placing objects (text and illustration) on web pages. Ask them questions such as:
   - *Where will you put the text?*
   - *In the centre?*
   - *On the right?*
   - *On the left?*
   - *In front/behind/next to?*
   - *Where will the photos go?*
   - *What colour will you use for the background/text?*

4 Distribute some large pieces of paper. Let the children draw a picture of their homepage.

5 Once the children have completed their web designs, put two groups together. One group describes their website to the other while that groups draws what they hear.

6 Hang up the website designs on the wall. Let the children look at them.

4.3 Our own web directory

LEVEL

Pre-intermediate and above

AGE

8 and above

TIME

45 minutes for setting up the activity, and then ongoing.

AIMS

To write clear descriptions of website content and to express opinions.

Language: Present simple tense.

MATERIALS

Worksheet 4.3, 'Web directory'.

IN CLASS

1 From the beginning of your class year, ask the children to fill out the Internet log in worksheet 4.3 to record every website they have visited and what day they were there.

2 When you are ready for your children to begin creating content, ask the children to look back at their Internet log and choose their three favourite sites. You may need to allow the children to return to some sites to refresh their memories.

3 Break up the class into small groups. From each of their three favourite websites, ask each child to choose one and write a description of its contents. Give lower-level students help by writing up questions such as:

–*Was the site easy to navigate?*
– *Did you like the colours?*
–*What's in it?*
–*What can you do?*
–*Are there pictures, videos, sound?*

4 If they haven't learnt already, demonstrate to the children how to create a hyperlink.

5 Each group then creates their own link page.

6 Underneath each link, the children type in their site descriptions from step 3. Have one child dictate the contents of the description, another type and a third check for correctness. Each child should have a chance to perform all three functions.

COMMENTS

This activity is a good bridge from web searching to practising the skill of setting links and working with a text editor.

4.4 Cartoon clip art

LEVEL

Elementary and above

AGE

8 and above

TIME

45 minutes

AIMS

To describe persons, places and things.

Language: Descriptive adjectives, present simple tense, *wh-*questions.

PREPARATION

Pre-select web links to cartoon character sites and create a handout with a list of the web addresses. See the suggestions in section 7 under 'Entertainment: Cartoons', page 114. You can also search for large clip art sites that generally contain lots of cartoons. See 'Clip art' in section 7, page 113.

IN CLASS

1 Ask the children if they like to watch cartoons. If possible show them pictures of some popular cartoon characters.

2 Tell the children that you have selected some websites where they can find cartoon characters. Distribute a handout with a list of web addresses.

3 Split the class up into small groups and have each group log on to one of the websites you distributed.

4 Ask the children to look at the characters on the site and to choose one character for each child in the group.

5 Ask the children to answer the following questions about the character:

   –*What's the character's name?*
   –*What's the name of the cartoon?*
   – *Is the character a person, monster, animal, etc.?*
   – *Describe the character. What colour is the character? Is it big or small? Is it happy or sad, mean or nice?*

6 Demonstrate to the children how to copy an image from a website. (See activity 1.5, 'Cut and paste', for instructions on how to do this.)

7 Ask the children to copy a picture of their chosen character and paste it to an individual word-processing document. (Make sure you have a word-processing application on your computer.)

8 Under the picture, have the children describe the cartoon character.

9 Print the pages with a colour printer and hang them up in your classroom.

VARIATION

Instead of creating word-processing documents, have each group create a PowerPoint presentation with one page for each cartoon character.

FOLLOW-UP

More advanced learners can create their own cartoon strip with the characters they have investigated. They can do this all online, creating speech bubbles with simple drawing tools, or they can simply copy and paste the pictures of the characters to a word-processing document, print it out, and fill in the dialogue by hand.

4.5   Dfilm

LEVEL

Elementary and above

AGE

10 and above

TIME

40 minutes + (depending on how many scenes and age of children)

AIMS

To create a short animated movie.

Language: Prepositions, adjectives, basic film vocabulary; the rest depends on the movie subject.

PREPARATION

Familiarize yourself with the Dfilm website. (See step 3.)

IN CLASS

1 Ask the children if they have a favourite movie. Write some of the movie titles on the board and elicit movie genres. For example:
   – The Matrix *is exciting. It's an action movie.*
   – Father of the Bride *is really funny. It makes me laugh. It's a comedy.*
   – Romeo and Juliet *is very sad. It's a love story.*
   – Star Wars *is about space. It's a science fiction movie.*

2 Split the class up into small groups per individual computer. Tell them they are going to make their own movie. Ask them to choose a genre.

3 Ask the children to open their web browser and type in the web address: *http://www.dfilm.com.*

4 Tell the children to click on 'Moviemaker'.

5 First the children will be asked to choose a background. Ask them where they think the background is located (in the bedroom, in a city, on a ship). Remind them of their choice of genre.

6 Tell the children to choose a 'sky'. The program will preview their choices.

7 Next the children must choose a plot. There are four choices. Let the children experiment. They can always go back and change their film.

8 Now the children can pick their character(s). Let them choose names. Ignore the information provided in the program.

9 At this point the children can write their dialogues. Ask them to create them on paper first. Circulate and check them or ask each group to bring them to you when they are finished.

10 Have the children type in their dialogues.

11 Let the children choose music for their movie. Ask them to describe the music with adjectives they know. Help them with some new ones, by writing them on the board.

12 Let the children select a title for their movie and appropriate background for the credits.

13 They send the finished film via email to their classmates.

14 Watch the films the children have created.

VARIATION 1	Send the Dfilm movie to your partner school or a friend or relative whose email address the children know (and you have checked for authenticity).
VARIATION 2	If you have a computer projector, show each movie to the entire class.
FOLLOW-UP 1	It is possible to create more than one scene. Let your children make a longer movie.
FOLLOW-UP 2	Rotate groups from one computer to another and let each new group create a new scene for the movie they find.
COMMENTS	This activity is dependent on one particular website. I hope it remains active.

4.6 King or Queen of the week

LEVEL	**Elementary and above**
AGE	**8 and above**
TIME	**30 minutes + to set up activity; ongoing.**
AIMS	**To talk about oneself.** **Language:** Present simple tense, *be*, *have*, *can*, and vocabulary depending on topics of interest.
MATERIALS	Scanner and/or digital camera.
PREPARATION	Prepare a 'King/Queen of the week' web page template for the children to work on. Write a letter to the parents describing the project.

IN CLASS

1 Tell your children that each week you will name one child King or Queen of the week.

2 Tell the children that the King or Queen of the week will prepare a presentation: *All about me*. This presentation will go on the class website.

3 Distribute a letter to their parents and an *All about me* worksheet to the children with questions about their home, family and interests to guide their preparation.

4 For homework the children must answer the questions and either provide photographs or draw pictures to illustrate their points.

5 Let the children sketch an outline of their web page. (See activity 4.2, ' "Design It" dictation'.) They must add captions for the images they provide. For example: *This is my dog, Lilli. Lilli is black. Lilli is ten.*

6 Create the page with the child. (See 'Web tutorials' in section 7, page 112.)

VARIATION 1

If you have trouble creating web pages, make a PowerPoint presentation instead.

VARIATION 2

Instead of the presentation *All about me*, let the children choose a subject of their choice. For instance, let them talk about their own hobbies or any collections they may have.

COMMENTS

You do not need an Internet Service Provider to post your page to. You can save web pages on your local computer.

4.7   Local museum

LEVEL

Intermediate and above

AGE

10 and above

TIME

40 minutes to set up activity; ongoing.

AIMS

To describe objects and how they relate to an understanding of a child's life.

Language: Varies according to topic, descriptive adjectives, present simple and simple past tenses.

IN CLASS

1 Ask the children to name some of the museums they visited on the web in activity 3.18, 'Museum quest'. Show them some printouts of objects in these museums. (See also activity 3.19, 'My favourite picture'.) Tell them that these objects tell the story of people or civilizations.

2 Tell the children that you now want them to create a museum or exhibition that will tell visitors about life in their home town.

3 Remind the children that the museums they have looked at all had different galleries and wings for various subjects. Tell them that they must divide their museum into sections as well. Put the following gallery headings on the board to get them started:
   – *Quick facts*
   – *Sites of interest*
   – *History*
   – *Events*

4 Now split the class into small groups. Let them choose one of the subjects. Either let the children explore online or bring material to class to browse through. This can also be a homework assignment and can be taught in collaboration with social studies teachers.

5 Once the children have had time to research their subject (the time is up to you), they must now choose three artefacts (objects) that symbolize what they have learned. These artefacts can be objects that you can digitize (drawings, sound, video, photographs) or objects that the children cut and paste from existing websites. Be sure to remind them that any information directly taken from another website needs to be acknowledged. (See section on copyright, page 21.)

6 Ask the children to write captions for their artefacts explaining why they are important and what they mean or signify. Circulate and give help where necessary.

7 Let the children decide the layout of the museum page. Let them use a web editor to create a local web page. If not, have them design the pages on paper and create the pages for them according to their designs. Save them to a local disk.

VARIATION 1

Make the museum project collaborative. Join one of the major keypal networks (see section 7, 'Finding partners, page 110) and initiate an international museum project with partners. Provide content for individual gallery wings such as the options listed above in step 3. Your class can be the curators and present the results on their website.

VARIATION 2

If the children are very young and do not have the English-language skills necessary for a full search, allow them to draw pictures and label them. You can then scan them into your computer.

FOLLOW-UP

Once the children have worked on one virtual museum, the museum concept can be transferred to any subject of interest. The opportunities for cross-curricular work are great.

4.8 Make a picture dictionary

LEVEL
Beginner and above

AGE
8 and above

TIME
90 minutes to set up activity; ongoing.

AIMS
To practise vocabulary.
Language: Whatever topics are being discussed in class.

MATERIALS
Digital camera and a scanner if possible. Picture dictionary.

PREPARATION
Create a web page template for the picture.

IN CLASS

1 Bring a picture dictionary into class. Show the children the dictionary and ask them if they have one at home.

2 Tell the children that you want them to create a picture dictionary on their computer for each topic that they learn, but first they need to know which words to use.

3 Choose your topics according to your curriculum and have the children brainstorm vocabulary. If the children are above the beginner stage, let them make mind maps and break down the topics into subgroups.

4 Assign a word to each child in the class. Ask them to draw a picture of it.

5 Scan the pictures into your computer. On one half of the page write the word in question and on the other paste the picture.

6 Call the children up to you in small groups and demonstrate what you did. If you have access to a computer projector, show the whole class at once.

7 In groups, the children create their picture dictionary pages.

8 On your class homepage, create hotlinks to the individual picture dictionary pages for example, alphabetically or according to topic.

9 At the end of each topic unit the children can create a new picture dictionary page as review.

VARIATION 1
Older children may prefer to cut and paste images from the Internet.

VARIATION 2
More advanced children may also write a definition under the picture. For example: *TIGER: a tiger is a large animal that lives in India.*

FOLLOW-UP
Older children can turn a picture dictionary into a topic collection with definitions, links to sites of interest, and student-generated materials.

4.9 Word search

LEVEL

Beginner and above

AGE

8 and above

TIME

Part 1: 40 minutes; Part 2: 20 minutes

AIMS

To practise vocabulary of a specific topic area; to listen to computer instructions.

Language: Depends on topic.

PREPARATION

Prepare a word search grid. This is easiest to do by creating a table in a word-processing document. See the example here. Fill in one copy and circle a few words you have found. You need to have an email address for each group of children.

Word search table for body parts

N	D	V	G	K	L	S	T
M	O	U	T	H	E	E	F
X	L	S	H	Y	W	F	G
N	U	B	E	S	C	I	Y
A	E	E	A	R	V	N	H
Z	O	C	D	N	X	G	R
T	K	E	K	N	E	E	J
F	O	O	T	A	I	R	W

EAR EYES FINGER FOOT HEAD LEG KNEE
MOUTH NOSE TOE

IN CLASS

Part 1

1 Show your children the word search you have created. Demonstrate which directions the words can be written.

2 Split the class up into small groups, each group at a computer terminal.

3 Tell the children you want them to make their own grids by creating a table using their word processor. Have them follow your instructions. Most word processors have similar features. In MS Word the instructions are:

– *Click on the 'Table'.*
– *Move your arrow over the word 'Insert'.*
– *Move your arrow to the right and click on 'Table'.*
– *Type in 8 under 'Number of columns' and 8 under 'Number of rows'.*
– *Click 'OK'.*

4 At this point a table will appear. The children must resize the table to turn it into a square. Show them how to drag and drop to resize.

5 Ask each group of children to choose a piece of paper with a topic you have covered in class. This could be animals, family, body parts, etc. For more advanced children this can be even more specific.

6 Ask the children to come up with ten words related to the topic. Check that the words are on topic.

7 Let the children key the words into the grid and fill in the remaining boxes with random letters.

8 For beginning and elementary students, have the children write the words to be found under the table. For more advanced students you can try letting them guess without the words.

9 Ask the children to save the document under the name of the topic they have chosen.

10 Ask the children to open their email program and send their grids as an attachment to their peers. This is most easily done by creating a class email list (see the section on 'Working with e-groups and discussion lists', page 18) and sending the message to all the addresses on the list at once. The sender will get the message too, but that doesn't matter.

Part 2

1 Ask one child in each group to check their email. Every child in the group should have received exactly the same grids.

2 Have the children conduct the word search. When they find a word, ask them to highlight the letters and change their colour.

3 When they are done, the children print their completed grid.

VARIATION 1	If you have a class website or group, post the grids there.
VARIATION 2	Create a relationship with English learners in other schools and/or countries and exchange grids.
VARIATION 3	If email or web options are not available, create the grids and have the groups of children exchange places and do the grids on the new terminal.

4.10 Switchzoo

LEVEL	**Beginner and above**
AGE	**7 and above (even younger possible)**
TIME	**Part 1: 45 minutes; Part 2: 45 minutes**
AIMS	**To create imaginary animals from existing ones** **Language:** Animals, parts of the body, descriptive adjectives, comparatives, superlatives, action verbs, question words; the rest depends on the fantasy of the children.

PREPARATION

Take time to familiarize yourself with the Switchzoo website (*http://www.switchzoo.com*) and the list of animals. You may want to make a poster or a handout with the steps required to use the site. Create one animal yourself (a *zebog*, for example) and print out a copy for each child. This activity works well before or after activity 3.15, 'My local habitat'.

IN CLASS

Part 1

1 Review animals with the children, using flashcards or other pictures you may have. Elicit some information about the animals:

   – *Are they big or small?*
   – *Have they got fur, a tail, claws?*
   – *Where do they live?*
   Introduce the nine primary Switchzoo animals. If they are new to the children, describe them.

2 Hold up the flashcards of two animals or write their names on the board, for example, *zebra* and *dog*. Using lots of exaggerated mime, ask the children: *What do you get if you mix a zebra and a dog?* Hold up the flashcards and indicate mixing, or draw two lines from the words on the board leading to point. Write the word: *Zebog.*

3 Ask the class: *Do you want to see a zebog?* Hand out pictures of your creature from the Switchzoo website.

4 Ask the children if they want to make their own animals too.

5 Split the children up into small groups and assign each group to a computer. Ask them to log on to *http://www.switchzoo.com*.

6 Demonstrate how the website functions—use a computer projector, or hand the children a series of screen shots and steps. It is a very easy site to use so the children will understand quickly.

7 Give the children a few minutes to experiment. Circulate among the groups and provide help where needed.

8 Ask each child (or group) to decide on a particular animal. Ask them to give the animal a name. When they print out the animal they can type a name under the picture. Ask them to write: *This is . . . .*

9 Print out the animals and let the children share them with their friends.

Part 2

1 Ask the children if they remember their fantasy animal. If you have a large class, split the class into small groups and have each group describe one animal.

2 Have the children write down their descriptions on a sheet of paper and glue the picture of the animal from Switchzoo to the top of the page.

3   Put all of the animals on a large sheet of colourful cardboard and
    hang it in the classroom.

FOLLOW-UP 1

Have the children write a story about their animals.

FOLLOW-UP 2

Instead of a paper and glue presentation, let the children create
their own 'web zoo' with a page for each animal. The children can
draw pictures of their own fantasy animals and you can scan them
into the computer and import them into a 'web zoo' template.

FOLLOW-UP 3

Let the children play the other games on the Switchzoo website.
Read the lesson plans submitted by teachers and consider trying
some of them out with your children.

4.11   Online cookbook

LEVEL

Pre-intermediate and above

AGE

8 and above

TIME

**Part 1: 90 minutes; Part 2: 90 minutes; ongoing, if doing
Follow-up.**

AIMS

To present favourite recipes on a web page.
Language: Food vocabulary, measurements, cooking terminology
and imperatives.

PREPARATION

Look up a simple recipe your children will be familiar with.

IN CLASS

Part 1

1   Write your chosen recipe up on the board. Tell the children: *This
    is my recipe for . . . .*

2   Ask the children what their favourite food is. Do they know how
    to make it? Do they know the recipe?

3   Tell the children that you want to make a class cookbook with all
    their favourite recipes. Each child must choose one recipe to
    write. They can either get it from friends and family or go to the
    Internet and search for it.

4   Go over the format for the recipes, for example:
    – *Title*   – *Portions*   – *Steps*
    – *Time for Preparation*   – *Ingredients*

5   Explain to the children that they will need to give the amounts
    required of each ingredient and the time for each step.

6   Have the children create a document with pictures of the dish
    and cooking instructions. They can either do this on the
    computer or by hand.

7 After class, scan the recipes or format them in HTML and link the individual recipes to a central recipe homepage. This homepage can be local or on the Internet.

Part 2

1 Choose a recipe to send to a partner school.

2 Have the partner school send your school a recipe.

3 Each class tries to cook the other school's recipe.

4 Via email the children comment on their impressions:

   –*Was it hard to cook?*
   – *Could they get all the ingredients?*
   – *If not, what did they do to improvize?*
   – *Did it taste good?*

VARIATION

Cooking in school may not be an easy thing to do. As a project, children can cook recipes at home and bring them to school for their classmates to try. The dishes can be photographed and these photographs used to illustrate the cookbook. (You can use a digital camera or scan real photographs.) As part of the Follow-up, you can send the photographs to your partner schools.

FOLLOW-UP

Start an international cookbook that the children can send on to partner schools around the world for contributions.

4.12 Reviews

LEVEL

Pre-intermediate and above

AGE

8 and above

TIME

60 minutes for initial activity; ongoing.

AIMS

To express opinions about books, music, or films, and to recount a story or plot.

Language: Adjectives, simple past tense, *like/don't like*, *why/because*; the degree of difficulty can be changed according to the level of the class.

MATERIALS

A book or CD which you particularly like. (See step 1.)

PREPARATION

Create a review template and put it in a place on the computer where the children can easily find it—in a folder labelled 'class templates', for example.

IN CLASS

1 Bring a book or CD to class. Show it to the children and say that you really liked it. Tell them a bit about it: what it contains, why you liked it.

2   Tell the children that you would like them to share some things they like with their friends around the world. They can choose music, books, films or even computer games.

3   Have the children write a short review of whatever they have chosen. They may write this by hand first.

4   Split the class into groups of 4–6 children. Explain to the children where they can find the review template and have them type in their reviews one after the other. One child reads the text, another types, and the rest check for mistakes.

5   Save the documents.

6   Tell the children that each week you will put a review on to the class website.

4.13 Serial story

LEVEL

Elementary and above

AGE

8 and above

TIME

For simple story: 90 minutes (not including photography, drawing and/or scanning); for web page design: 90 minutes.

AIMS

To create a dialogue.

Language: Depends on context.

IN CLASS

1   Show the children examples of serial picture stories as often appear in youth or teen magazines.

2   Have the children create a storyboard where they design their photo story, frame by frame. In doing so the children must decide on:

–*Who are the characters?*
–*What is the setting?*
– *How does the story begin?*
–*What happens in the middle?*
–*What is the resolution?*

3   Having established the storyboard, the children must now write dialogue for the characters.

4   Children now take a digital camera and photograph the scenes. If no digital camera is available, they can scan photos or cartoon drawings they have made.

5   The children line the photographs up on a web page. Using a computer drawing tool, create speech bubbles and have the children write in their dialogue.

VARIATION 1

The photo story can be an ongoing project like a soap opera. The children can regularly change their roles—photographer, web designer, dialogue writer.

5 Electronic portfolios

One of the most exciting applications of technology in the classroom is the electronic portfolio. Portfolios, electronic or standard, are playing an increasingly important role in assessment throughout education as teachers move away from a teach-test-teach model towards a type of assessment that can portray progress over time.

What is a portfolio? It is a rather elusive term. For the purposes of this book, a portfolio is simply 'a purposeful collection of a student's work'. Through a portfolio, teachers, parents, and most importantly, the children themselves are able to track the learning process and see how they grow. For more detailed information on portfolios, see the book *Assessing Young Learners* in this series.

Electronic portfolios are very practical in this regard.

They take up less space.
Collections of student work can be very bulky. By digitizing materials or working on a computer from the start, you can have the same results in a more convenient form that will not take up extra classroom space.

They are easy to modify.
Once materials are digitized, they can be worked on and changed with relative ease. This gives the children more flexibility in using the portfolio and saves time. For example, if the children draw a picture, it can be modified and saved under a different name, preserving the preceding version as well, without having to start from scratch.

They are more permanent and robust.
Standard paper portfolios will become frayed over time through handling and transport. Electronic portfolios on the other hand stay in the same state as the first day they were used and are always 'brand new'. You should, of course, back up the portfolios on a regular basis.

Creating an electronic portfolio

There are many different portfolio models being implemented around the world. A discussion of these models would go beyond the scope of this book. The focus here is on the specifics of creating electronic display portfolios. This portfolio model can be broken down into the following steps:

– collecting
– organizing
– evaluating
– presenting

Collecting

Before you can introduce the portfolio to your students, you need to decide what you intend to collect. Most of the activities in this book have a portfolio application. Be sure to include your children in the decision-making process. Portfolios should also not only be tied to school or national standards, but should also reflect the interests of the individual students. While some aspects of the portfolio may be mandatory, allow your children the freedom to pick and choose what they feel is important, or something they are particularly fond of. Making decisions about their portfolio will help children to take responsibility for their learning in general.

Selection of portfolio items will also be determined by the technological options at your disposal. Assess your technology resources and measure them against the goals of your portfolio.

– Do you have a scanner to digitize student work? If you don't, you will not be able to include handwritten material or drawings.
– Do you have software to record digital audio and video? If not, you will be limited to 'electronic paper'.
– Is your Internet connection fast enough to download images and documents without long waiting times and excessive cost?

If you have neither scanner nor media software, portfolio work will need to be done on the computer from the start. Of course this assumes that you have a good word-processing application installed.

Alongside the technical requirements you need to assess your computer skills as well.

– Do you have the background to create a very elaborate portfolio framework?
– Do your children share these skills? If not, will you have the time to teach yourself and/or the children without sacrificing valuable classroom time?

Each portfolio in a class should have a similar look and feel. They should also include certain key components that you can create as templates for your class. Basic components of all portfolios are:

– *Title page*
– *Table of contents* (This is very important to ensure that the viewer can trace the history of the child's learning.)
– *Personal information page* (A place where the children say a little bit about themselves, their likes and dislikes, and perhaps include a photograph.)

Organizing

Once you have determined what kind of portfolio materials to collect, you still need to decide on how to organize the documents. The electronic environment presents a multitude of options.

– *Individual portfolios*
  Each child has their own portfolio as a separate electronic file.
– *Portfolio page with links*
  If you can post documents to the web or a local LAN network, each child can create their individual portfolio files and link them via a central portfolio homepage.
– *Databases*
  Modern database applications allow you to create electronic filing cabinets that can be searched according to multiple criteria. All your children's materials can be collected in one place and be called up according to customized criteria. These databases have Internet capabilities and can be integrated into a class website.

Evaluating

Portfolios are assessment tools and thus we need to consider how they are evaluated.

– If you work in a school which follows a state curriculum, you may link entries in the portfolios to specific aspects of this curriculum which may appear on an official website.
– If you have more freedom in designing your syllabus, you can provide a link to your own 'objectives' documents.
– Each portfolio item can also be evaluated according to a specific 'rubric' or scoring system, which can be compiled in a separate document or become part of the portfolio itself.
– Finally, there is student self-assessment. You may want to design checklists for the children to fill out at certain times of the year. When filed by date, the children can follow their own progress.

Presenting

Having established a portfolio, you need to think about how it will be presented. In the case of electronic portfolios, this is almost always synonymous with the question of where it is stored. There are a number of different options to consider:

– *Floppy disks*
  This is probably an unrealistic option unless your portfolio is limited to simple word-processing documents. Documents that contain substantial graphics, sound or video will be far too big to fit on a floppy disk.
– *Zip Disks*
  Zip disks are external disks with a far greater storage capacity than a floppy disk. Zip disks require separate zip disk drives and that costs money. Also, although a zip disk can probably store your

entire classes portfolios, each child would want their own to show to parents and they would need a zip drive to view it.

— *CD/RW*

Rewriteable CD's are a good option for displaying portfolios. Most computers are equipped with built-in CD-Rom drives and rewriteable drives are not expensive, nor are the CD's themselves.

— *LAN networks*

If your school or organization has its own intranet or local area network, you can place all your class's portfolios on your local server. Anybody with access to the network can then view the portfolios. See, however, the note about password protection on page 14.

— *Internet*

Finally, you can post your portfolios to the web. You will need to check with your Internet Service Provider or host about space for your documents. This is, of course, a very exciting option for the children: it really makes them feel 'published'.

6 The Internet as a teacher resource

The activities in this book have focused on how your students can use the Internet in the EFL classroom. However, this book would be incomplete without a mention of the most common use of the Internet in EFL—teachers searching for resources to use in traditional, unconnected classrooms.

The Internet is teeming with sites offering lesson plans for every subject ever taught in primary school. While few of these sites are directly aimed at young learners of English as a foreign language, there are scores of ESL sites with activities that can be modified to the more limited language environment of EFL. Even more valuable in my mind are what I term 'content sites'. These sites are devoted to themes and topics which young learners find interesting and motivating. They can provide the spice for an otherwise traditional lesson in the form of pictures, sounds or simply new information. The options are endless.

And that is the biggest problem. You can never search the entire Internet. Every search engine you use is merely looking through a selection of websites, never the Internet in its totality. It takes discipline to use the Internet effectively as a resource tool and to pick and choose rather than browse aimlessly, bouncing from one link to the next.

In order to narrow the search process for you, section 7 lists a selection of sites that have proved valuable and easy to use. But first here are some tips on 'mining' the web.

Know what you are looking for

The more clearly you know what you want, presumably the easier it will be to find. Are you looking for a specific place or person, or are you just hoping to get a broad introduction to a topic? If your subject is very broad, it makes sense to look at a web directory like 'Yahoo!' where websites are placed in searchable categories. You move through the categories, getting ever more specific. The problem here is that it is hard to predict how your information may be classified. Each search engine has its own unique criteria. This gets easier if you use a more specific subdirectory. See 'Search engines: general' in section 7, page 111, for some good directories or portals.

Searching without directories is generally more successful if you have a clear idea of what you are looking for. Type in *Disneyworld* and you will get all the websites available with that word in them. This, of course, could lead to an overwhelming amount of information and anything from jobs at *Disneyworld*, to local hotels, or a calendar of events.

You can limit your search quite easily by using 'Boolean logic'. Boolean logic uses words known as 'operators' to link information. The operators are:

– AND
– NOT
– OR

Most search engines automatically add the AND between words of a search. Thus if you type in *Disneyland opening hours*, the search engine will select all pages which include these keywords. On the other hand if you use the Boolean operator NOT, as in a search such as *Disneyland* NOT *hotel*. All sites with the keyword *hotel* will be omitted. Finally, if you use the operator OR—*Disneyland* OR *hotel*— the search engine will look for sites that contain either *Disneyland* or *hotel*. The selected sites can contain both, but don't have to.

By varying your search according to these criteria, you can approach information from a number of different directions and narrow your results without having to work with different keywords. Explore the 'Advanced search' function that many search engines have.

Distinguish between a portal and a content site

As the name suggests, a portal is a gateway to information, not usually a place where you will find concrete information itself. In other words, you will find a description of links, sometimes in depth and other times with no real comment at all. Such portals can be very helpful, but all too often a click on a portal link leads to another portal or link list. I try and keep to a 'two-click' rule. If I am not at a content page after the second click, I move elsewhere.

Organize your Bookmarks or Favourites well

Bookmarks are a very handy tool for organizing information as long as you sort them in a logical fashion. What that means will depend on your own preferences, of course. Filing with an Internet browser works in pretty much the same way as any Windows or Macintosh desktop—documents are placed into folders. These folders can, in turn, be placed within other folders creating multiple layers of sorting information. Thus you could have a master folder for your course and, within the folder, embedded folders on each unit or topic you are teaching.

Here are a few tips on organizing your Bookmarks or Favourites:

Don't Bookmark everything
Be selective. Too many Bookmarks, no matter how well organized, will lead to clutter. Also, bear in mind that many sites (especially portals) will inevitably reference the same links. You will never get to the 'end' of the Internet, so limit yourself to a few key link collections.

Sort your Bookmarks immediately
Don't wait until later. You may forget what the content of the link is. The name or address of a link is not very revealing. This means that you will have to spend extra time re-reading links to find out where they belong.

Create a 'View later' folder
Use this folder for links you don't have a chance to fully evaluate before filing. This will keep needless clutter out of your other folders.

Put your most frequently used Bookmarks on your browser's tool bar
Both Internet Explorer and Netscape let you do this. Consult the online help for exact instructions.

Get rid of dead links on a regular basis
You can do this manually if you don't have too many links, or with a link-validating utility program.

Save your Bookmarks
If your computer crashes, you could lose all your information.

7 Useful Internet addresses

The information provided here is up-to-date and the links are all live at the time of going to press. The Internet is, however, constantly changing, with some websites becoming inactive or unobtainable, while new ones appear on a daily basis. For more up-to-date information, consult the book's website at *http://www.oup.com/elt/teacher/rbt.* We also welcome readers' feedback and suggestions.

Inclusion in these lists does not necessarily mean that the author or publisher of this book endorse their content.

Note that a few activities (3.5, 3.15, 4.5, and 4.10) are dependent on particular websites. If these go down, then the activity will not work or will need substantial modification. The book's website will seek to repair any damage of this kind.

You should also note that many of the sites listed will contain advertisements. If this is a problem in your school environment, you should make a point of checking the appropriacy of the adverts before recommending the sites to your students.

This section is in two parts. The first part is 'general' and contains references to websites, portals, and search engines that are useful for all kinds of activities on the Internet. The second part is 'content': this contains references to resources on specific topics.

General

Creating websites

Webmonkey
http://hotwired.lycos.com/webmonkey/kids/
This is an easy-to-understand tutorial site for creating web pages with your children. There is also a strictly adult version at the webmonkey homepage. Click beginners to get started.

Trackstar
http://trackstar.scrtec.org/
This site allows you to turn your Bookmarks into a table of contents with previews of sites.

Filamentality
http://www.kn.pacbell.com/wired/fil/index.html
Like Trackstar, a way to generate meaningful activities on the web. May be a bit above the level of our students. Blue Web'n web also part of this site.

Internet In-fusiasm
http://www.ptnet.lsu.edu/pam/PhII/Infus_tasks.html
An easy to follow list to Internet tools and resources.

Web66
http://web66.coled.umn.edu/
A very useful site on all technological aspects of working with the Internet, including tutorials. Also has an international registry of schools that are online.

E-cards

http://scholastic.com/kids/cards
http://www.e-cards.com
http://www.animatedcards.org/
http://www.bluemountain.com/
http://www.e-cards.com/site/
http://www.marlo.com/

Educational links: general

American Library Association
http://www.ala.org/Content/NavigationMenu/ALSC/Great_Web_Sites_for_Kids/Great_Web_Sites_for_Kids.htm
A very rich resource with masses of curriculum-related and general information. It features a 'Website of the month'.

Blue Web'n
http://www.kn.pacbell.com/wired/bluewebn/index.html
An excellent collection of web resources, also by content area.

Community Learning Network
http://www.cln.org/subject_index.html
A great one-stop site with links to projects, e-cards, theme-based lessons and more tech-related children's stuff.

Education World
http://www.education-world.com
Not only tech, but also lesson-plan ideas on everything under the sun.

Enchanted Learning
http://www.enchantedlearning.com/Home.html
A great collection of activities for young learners. Check out the online multilingual picture dictionary. My favourite site.

Shrock Guide
http://school.discovery.com/schrockguide/index.html
A huge site with information on all aspects of education especially the use of technology in the classroom. Lots of good downloadable material for assessment.

Teaching Ideas
http://www.teachingideas.co.uk
UK site with general teaching ideas and a handy collection of ICT activities, including a very simple introduction to the Internet.

Educational links: EFL

IATEFL Young Learners' Special Interest Group
http://www.countryschool.com/ylsig/
This is probably the most comprehensive site specifically aimed at YL-EFL.

The Internet TESL Journal
http://iteslj.org/
Interesting articles and a huge link section.

Eastern Valley Teacher Development Site
http://www.yarden.ac.il/chinuch/english/new_efl.htm
A very useful and clearly designed site.

ElEaston
http://eleaston.com/
A big site devoted to languages. Includes quiz generators and a large section on using the Internet, with tutorials.

Dave's EFL Café
http://www.eslcafe.com
A very popular site with EFL teachers.

E-groups

Yahoo
http://groups.yahoo.com/

MSN
http://groups.msn.com/

Topica
http://www.topica.com/

Email: free services

Yahoo
http://www.yahoo.com

Start (Australia)
http://www.start.com.au/

Hotmail
http://www.msn.com/
Click on the hotmail button.

Finding partners

Global Schoolhouse
http://www.gsn.org/
A big list of web projects and possible partners as well as resources and technology information.

I*Earn
http://www.iearn.org/
One of the largest and most stable international web project and
partner organisations. You must pay to be a member, unless your
school is already one.

Teaching.com
http://www.teaching.com/
Hosts Keypals and IECC, databases where students and teachers
can find partners.

Games and activity generators

Quia
http://www.quia.com/
Lets you create games and quizzes. Pay-site but has 30 days free
introductory period.

Search engines: children-specific

Kidsclick Search engine
http://sunsite.berkeley.edu/KidsClick!/

Yahoo's Yahooligans
http://www.yahooligans.com

Ask Jeeves
http://www.ajkids.com

Ivy's Search Engines for Kids
http://www.ivyjoy.com/rayne/kidssearch.html
An extensive list of children-friendly search engines and resource
sites.

Search engines: general

http://www.altavista.com
http://www.google.com/
http://www.yahoo.com/
http://search.msn.com/
http://www.lycos.com/
http://www.ask.com/

Typing programs

http://www.learn2type.com
http://www.mavisbeacon.com
http://www.typingmaster.com
http://www.schoolblogs.com/isdweblog/
http://www.diaryland.com/
http://www.blog-city.com/
http://www.blogger.com

Webcams

Earthcam for Kids
http://www.earthcamforkids.com/

Web hosting: free services

Matmice
http://www.matmice.com
This free site lets children create their own websites and also hosts them. In simple steps, the children can create a site and preview it in minutes. This is great place to start children on web creation projects.

EON Webpagemaker
http://www.e-o-n.org/htmauler/admin.html
Another site where you can create your own web page in a matter of steps.

Geocities
http://www.geocities.com
Yahoo's free web hosting. Easy to use but lots of advertising.

Weblogs

http://www.schoolblogs.com/isdweblog/
http://www.diaryland.com/
http://www.blog-city.com/
http://www.blogger.com

Web tutorials

Pagetutor
http://www.pagetutor.com/

Webteacher
http://www.webteacher.org/windows.html

Content

Animals

Nature Photos
http://www.mynaturephotos.com/index.htm
Nice photos and a place where your learners could place their own.

San Diego Zoo
http://www.sandiegozoo.org/kids/index.html
Check out the animal profiles. Lots of extras. Language is simple. Children can master it with support.

Tiger Information Center
http://www.5tigers.org/Directory/kids.htm
Lots of facts about tigers written in very clear and simple language. See the section called 'Tigers talk back' for your lower level students.

Discovery Channel
http://animal.discovery.com/
All the popular television shows, live cams, videos, photos. Lots to look at.

Habitats
http://library.thinkquest.org/11922/habitats/habitats.htm
Nice site on habitats that is actually a web project itself.

Switchzoo
http://www.switchzoo.com
Morphing animals online. Lots of fun and a bit crazy.

Birthdays

Time capsule
http://dmarie.com/timecap/
Easy to use site with information on headlines, top songs, famous people born on your birthday.

What day of the week
http://www.onlineconversion.com/dayborn.htm
Calculates what day of the week you were born on.

The day I was born project
http://www.stphilipneri.org/teacher/dayiwasborn/
An Internet project with international participation. It has almost only English-speaking schools involved so it may be a bit too demanding in terms of language. However, it offers a good model to create your own version of the project.

Clip art

http://www.theclipartportal.com/
A good selection of links to start exploring.

http://www.awesomeclipartforkids.com/
http://www.kidsdomain.com/clip/
http://school.discovery.com/clipart/

Countries and cultures

Currency converter
http://www.oanda.com/convert/classic

Country reports
http://www.countryreports.org/
A very practical site that offers a picture of a county's flag, a map and even a link to its national anthem as a midi file. There is a lot more detailed information as well, which more advanced and older students (10 and above) will understand and find useful.

Distances
http://www.pvv.ntnu.no/~hallsteo/world/
This is a practical site since you can choose locations from menus, making mistakes less likely.

Distance conversion
http://www.cloos.com/content_convert_distances.html
Allows you to convert down to an inch or centimeter—also has nautical distances.

Houses
http://www.hgpho.to/wfest/house/house-e.html

Entertainment

Cartoons
http://www.cartoonnetwork.com
http://www.nick.com
http://pbskids.org

Movies
US-based
http://movies.yahoo.com/showtimes/showtimes.html
http://www.hollywood.com/

UK-based
http://www.cinemaclock.com/clock/ont/London.html

Australia-based
http://www.movieguide.com.au/

Music
BBC Radio 3
http://www.bbc.co.uk/radio3/games/index.shtml
A beat machine to compose your own music and lots of fun music games.

mtv
http://www.mtv.com
Find out about everything about all the hottest new bands and singers. You can also watch videos. You might want to look at this site as a teacher so you can keep up with what your children are talking about.

Karaoke of popular children's songs
http://www.canadiankids.net/ck/singalong.jsp
This is great for teachers if you don't know the music to a song text. Also see the Canadian kids homepage for other good ideas.

http://www.lyrics.com/
http://www.azlyrics.com/
Two good sites for finding lyrics to popular songs. Don't worry if the children can't understand all the words. They will be eager to translate—it's cool. However, exercise utmost care when allowing them to choose songs, as many popular tunes are not really appropriate for children's ears. Parents who don't understand English may be shocked to learn what the children are actually listening to—even if the children don't really know what it all means.

Facts and figures

Factmonster
http://www.factmonster.com
A great source for children-oriented facts, written in a clear simple style and with an easy navigation.

Fun stuff

Bustamove
http://www.bustamove.com/
A site with dance animation. Register and choose single steps or whole dances or have children combine their moves to create their own dance.

Kidsfun Canada
http://www.kidsfuncanada.com/en/
A fun site with animated fairy tales, lots of games and activities and a children's search engine:
http://www.childrencanada.com/

Dfilm
http://www.dfilm.com/index_main.html
Really fun site which allows you to choose characters and backgrounds and write a short dialogue for an animated film which you can send as an email.

Netfundu
http://www.netfundu.com/
A pretty bright and colourful site from India that has a great section on movies and music stars. The language is a bit tough, but the content will excite children 10 and up.

Rhymezone
http://www.rhymezone.com/
Type in a word and it finds a rhyme. Great for seeing how different spellings sound the same. Comes with definitions as well and little extras.

The Yuckiest Site on the Net
http://yucky.kids.discovery.com/
Learn about bugs and some fairly unpleasant aspects of the human body. Strange, but certainly appealing to your children.

Games

http://www.gameskidsplay.net/
Hundreds of games. Ideal to find interesting options for your 'Elympics'.

Greek myths

http://library.thinkquest.org/CR0210901/
Click on Greek mythology. You can then make a cross-curricular link to the Greek Gods and let the children read their stories.
http://www.mythweb.com/gods/Zeus.html

Museums

Museums Online
http://musee-online.org
Links to 37,000 thousand museums worldwide with a directory by type of museum.

Metropolitan Museum New York
http://www.metmuseum.org/collections/index.asp

The British Museum
http://www.thebritishmuseum.ac.uk/compass/
This is a link to a child-dedicated site.

Children's Museums
http://www.childrensmuseums.org
A list of links to children's museums.

Natural world

The World's Great Rivers
http://cgee.hamline.edu/rivers/Resources/river_profiles/
General information on rivers. Best used in conjunction with another site such as the Factmonster river page:
http://www.factmonster.com/ipka/A0001779.html
and photos and maps of rivers which you can get by searching for images in your search engine.

Volcanoes
http://volcano.und.nodak.edu/vwdocs/kids/kids.html
This is the pre-eminent volcano site I can find.

National Geographic Society
http://www.nationalgeographic.com/

Weather links
http://illiniweather.com/pages/kids_weather_links.htm
A really useful set of links to weather reports and also educational sites dealing with weather phenomena.

Weather for children
http://www.ucar.edu/educ_outreach/webweather/
This site has some really fun weather games. It would be a great cross-curricular resource. You may need to help the children in their mother tongue, but after an introduction the children will be able to play the games independently.

USA Today weather
http://www.usatoday.com/weather/forecast/wglobe.htm
This site has a very clear and simple navigation

Shopping

International Association of Department Stores
http://www.iads.org/HTML/indexs.htm
Worldwide list of department stores

Dillards (USA)
http://www.dillards.com/info/sitemap.jsp

Harrods (UK)
http://www.harrods.com/

Target (USA)
http://www.target.com

David Jones (Australia)
http://www.davidjones.com.au/home.jsp

Space

Sites with general information on the Solar System:
http://www.frontiernet.net/~kidpower/astronomy.html
http://mercury.nineplanets.org:8011/tnp4kids/
http://www.dustbunny.com/afk/planets/planets.htm
http://spacekids.com/
http://library.thinkquest.org/CR0210901/
http://space.jpl.nasa.gov/
This is the Space Simulator. It has lots of links to other areas of the virtually endless NASA website.

http://www.exploratorium.edu/ronh/age/index.html
http://www.exploratorium.edu/ronh/weight/
Age and weight in Space. Be sure to go to the Exploratorium homepage as well. It is a fun and creative resource for everything to do with science.

http://www.skyviewcafe.com
An interactive online planetarium. Not too hard to use with a bit of help from the teacher.

Sports

Football Association (England)
http://www.FA-Premier.com

European Soccer Federation
http://www.uefa.com/

World Soccer Federation
http://www.fifa.com/index.html

NBA Basketball
http://www.nba.com

American Football
http://www.nfl.com

Time and date

Maps and time zones

http://www.maps.com/explore/
All kinds of maps including aerial images of the USA. Country facts and a time zone map and calculator.

http://www.timeanddate.com/date/
List of calendar and time calculators. Check out the duration calculator that lets you determine time elapsed between any two dates.

http://www.constructionweblinks.com/Resources/Reference__Resources/ Time__Date__Calendars/time__date__calendars.html
Page with links to time zone and calendar sites.

The Earth calendar

http://www.earthcalendar.net/index.php
This is a calendar of holidays around the world, conveniently searchable by date, country, and religion.

Calendars through the ages
http://webexhibits.org/calendars/
Calendars of different religions and interesting facts about calendars in general.

Transportation

Subways and rapid transit
http://www.reed.edu/~reyn/transport.html
Maps, schedules, and information on mass transit around the world. Some of the links are dead. You need to do a bit of research here, but still better than searching for each subway system individually.

Travel
http://www.expedia.com
http://www.travelocity.com

Connect the words and the pictures.

computer

monitor

keyboard

mouse

printer

disk drive

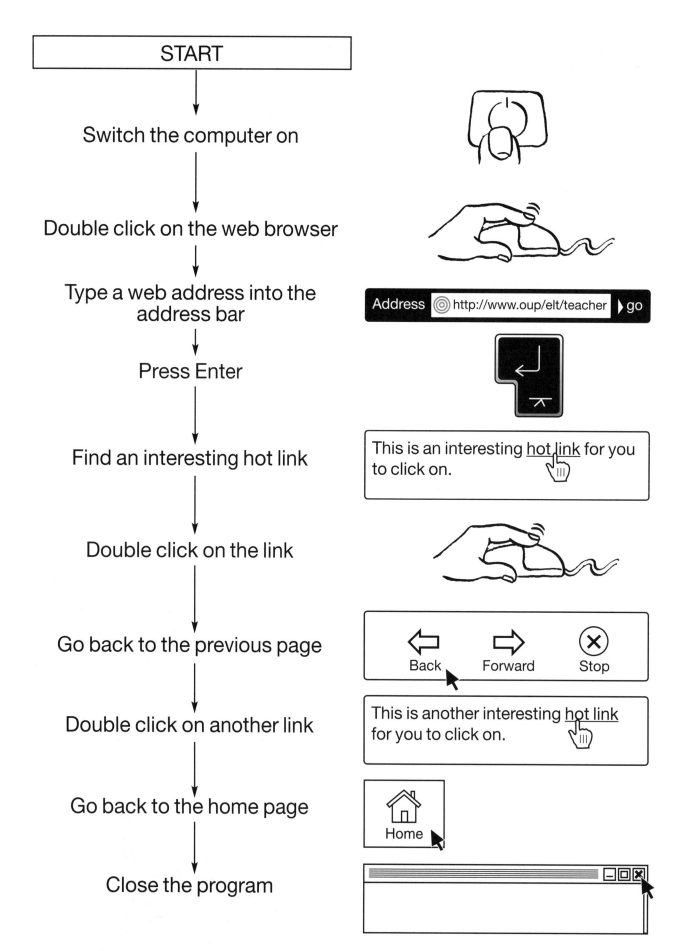

START

Switch the computer on

Double click on the web browser

Type a web address into the address bar

Address ⊚ http://www.oup/elt/teacher ▶ go

Press Enter

Find an interesting hot link

This is an interesting hot link for you to click on.

Double click on the link

Go back to the previous page

⬅ Back   ⮕ Forward   ⊗ Stop

Double click on another link

This is another interesting hot link for you to click on.

Go back to the home page

🏠 Home

Close the program

Name _____ **Class** _____ **Date** _____

Address of website looked at: _____ http://www. _____

What it is about: _____

_____

What I liked most

- [ ] content (text)
- [ ] activities/games
- [ ] links
- [ ] content (pictures)
- [ ] format/design
- [ ] other _____

My mind map of the site

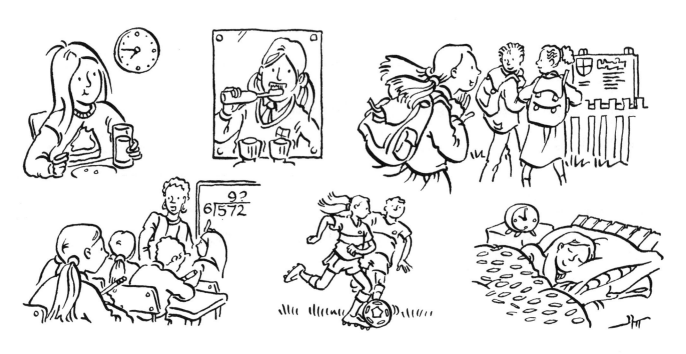

Day of the week _____

Time	Activity

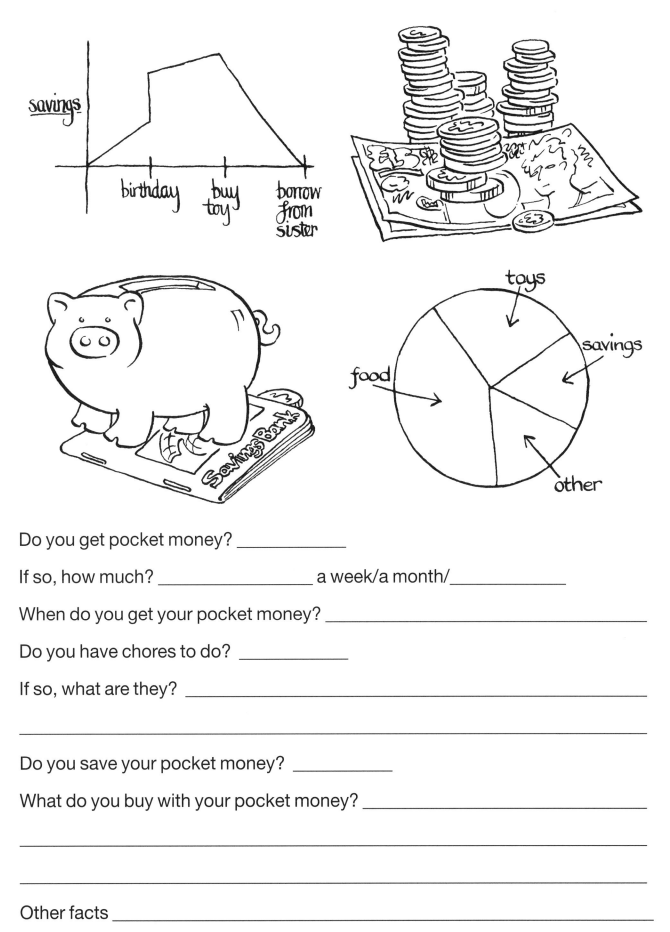

Do you get pocket money? _____

If so, how much? _____ a week/a month/_____

When do you get your pocket money? _____

Do you have chores to do? _____

If so, what are they? _____

_____

Do you save your pocket money? _____

What do you buy with your pocket money? _____

_____

_____

Other facts _____

WEEK FROM _____ TO _____

CITY	Sun		Mon		Tues		Thurs		Fri		Sat		Sun	
	W	T	W	T	W	T	W	T	W	T	W	T	W	T
Rome														

sunny

cloudy

rain

windy

changeable

snowy

W = weather

T = temperature …°C/…°F

The highest temperature of the week was in _____

The lowest temperature of the week was in _____

Events ↓ Names →				
long jump				
50 metre run				
egg and spoon race				
sack race				

Household goods	Quantity	Price

Dairy	Quantity	Price

Meat	Quantity	Price

Snacks & sweets	Quantity	Price

Other	Quantity	Price

Fruit	Quantity	Price

Vegetables	Quantity	Price

Bread & cereal	Quantity	Price

My town

Name of the town

Population: _____

How to get there:

_____
_____
_____
_____

Location

Tourist attractions

1 _____
2 _____
3 _____
4 _____

Where to stay

Weather

spring _____
summer _____
autumn _____
winter _____

| CALENDAR | DAYS IN A YEAR | NAMES OF THE DAYS | MONTHS IN A YEAR | NAMES OF THE MONTH | BASED ON | | | COUNTRIES THAT USE THIS CALENDAR |
					SUN	MOON	EARTH	
Christian/ Gregorian	365	Monday Tuesday Wednesday	12	January February March				
Islamic								
Chinese								
Mayan								

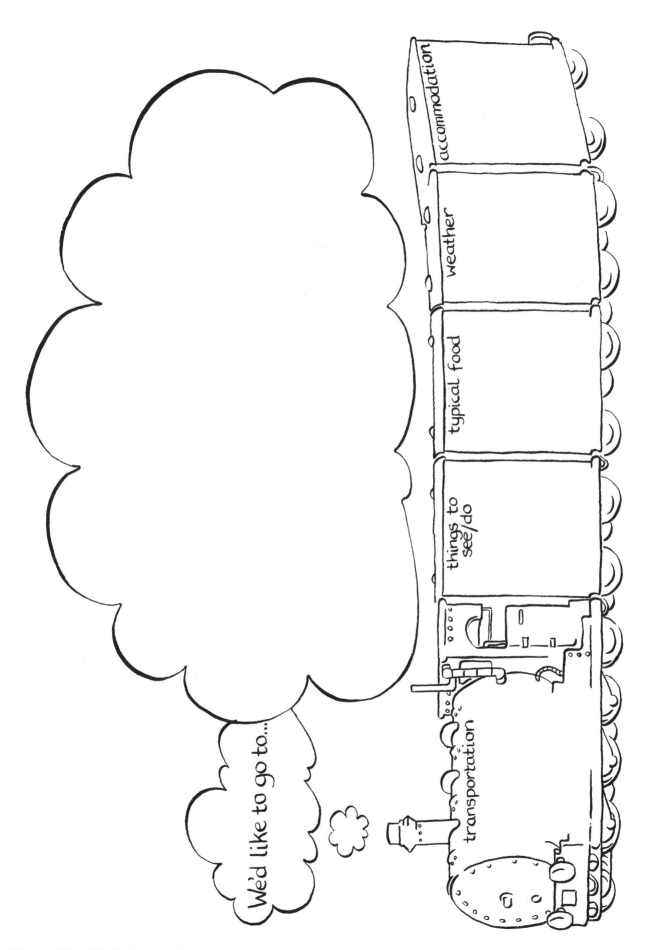

How far is it ...

... from	... to?	My guess	True distance

Name of metro system _____

City _____

How many lines does the system have? _____

What colours are the lines? _____

_____

_____

Do the lines connect at a central station? _____

How many stations are there on the shortest line? _____

How many stations are there on the longest line? _____

Which station has the most lines going through it? _____

To get from _____ to _____ takes _____ minutes.

To get from _____ to _____ change trains at _____ .

3RD FLOOR	furniture, toys, sports
2ND FLOOR	men's wear
1ST FLOOR	women's wear, swimwear, children's clothes
GROUND FLOOR	cosmetics, stationery, books, newspapers, china, glass
BASEMENT	household goods, cooking, electrical goods, computers

Name of store _____

Location _____

Opening hours _____

How many departments has the store got? _____

What are they? _____

_____

_____

In which department can you find the following?

a girl's dress _____

perfume _____

a basketball _____

a computer _____

a man's suit _____

Choose one of these items and write down who makes it and what it costs.

made by _____   cost _____

Name of river _____

Continent _____

Where does the river begin? _____

Which countries does it flow through? _____

_____

How long is the river? _____

Do other rivers flow into it? _____

If so, which rivers? _____

_____

Are there cities on the river? _____

If so, which cities? _____

_____

What languages are spoken along the river? _____

_____

Other interesting things about the river _____

_____

Name of volcano _____

What continent is it on? _____

Which country is it in? _____

How high is it? _____

When did it last erupt? _____

Was there any damage?_____

If so, what was the damage? _____

_____

_____

Were any people hurt or killed?_____

_____

Is the volcano still active? _____

Other interesting things about the volcano _____

_____

_____

At the _____ **Museum**

TITLE _____

Name of the artist _____

Date of creation _____

Place of creation _____

☐ It is a painting.   ☐ It is a sculpture.   ☐ It is a photograph.

It portrays _____

☐ I like it.   ☐ I don't like it.

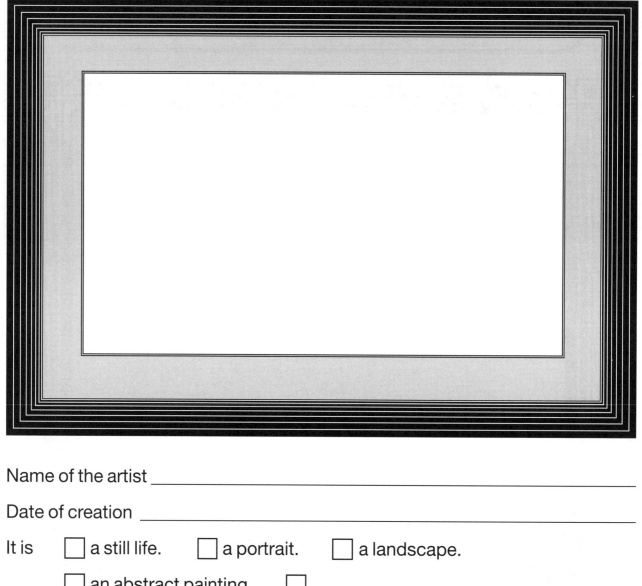

Name of the artist _____

Date of creation _____

It is   ☐ a still life.   ☐ a portrait.   ☐ a landscape.

☐ an abstract painting.   ☐ _____ .

Colours in the picture _____

Shapes in the picture _____

In the front of the picture I can see _____

_____

At the back of the picture I can see _____

_____

I like it because _____

_____

LEVEL 1

How many planets are there?

What are their names?

Which is the smallest planet?

Which is the biggest planet?

Which planet is nearest Earth?

Which planet is nearest the Sun?

How old is our Solar System?

How big is the Sun?

LEVEL 2

Choose a planet:

How far is it from the Sun?

Is it bigger or smaller than Earth?

How far is it from Earth?

How long does it take to orbit the Sun?

How long does it take for Earth to orbit the Sun?

How many satellites/moons does it have?

LEVEL 3

What is a light year?

What is a black hole?

What are gamma rays?

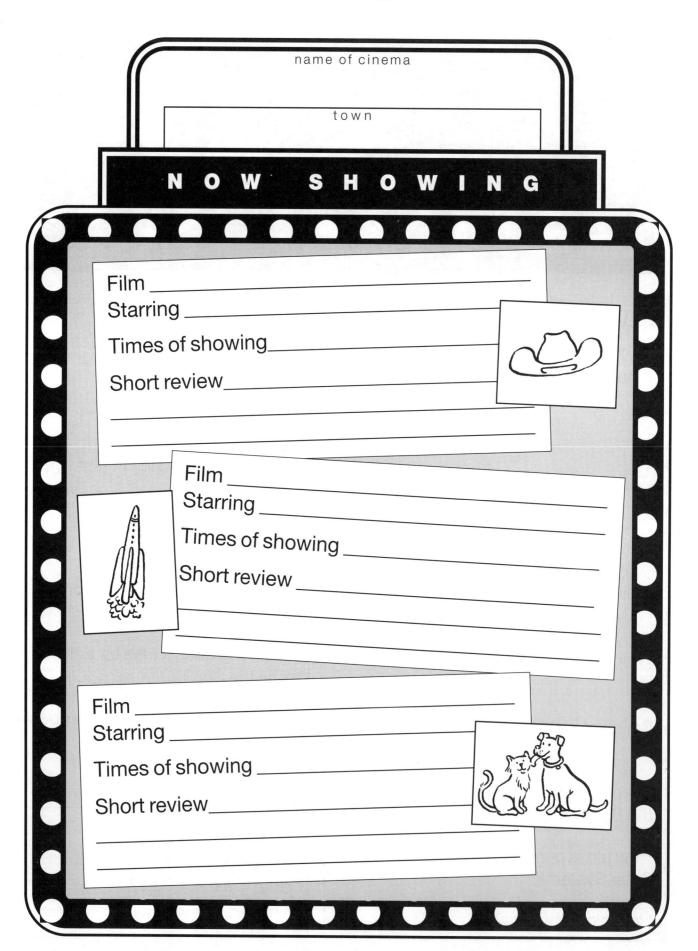

name of cinema

town

N O W   S H O W I N G

Film _____

Starring _____

Times of showing _____

Short review _____

_____

Film _____

Starring _____

Times of showing _____

Short review _____

_____

Film _____

Starring _____

Times of showing _____

Short review _____

_____

My favourite team

their emblem

Name of team _____

Sport _____

Country _____ Date _____

Colour of kit _____

Name of home ground _____

Their best player(s) _____

_____

Have they ever won the league/championship? _____

When did they win the league/championship? _____

What place are they in now? _____

Who did they play in their last game? _____

Who won and what was the score? _____

Who are they playing next? _____

Who will win, do you think? _____

Name of website		
address (URL)		
What is the site about?		
What kinds of illustration did you see?	☐ drawings ☐ photos ☐ charts ☐ movies ☐ animations ☐ other	☐ drawings ☐ photos ☐ charts ☐ movies ☐ animations ☐ other
Did the site have sound?		
Was the site easy to move around/understand?		
What did you like?		
What did you not like?		

Index

Language

This is not an exhaustive list. Most activities can be modified or expanded to include many more language items.

Index of vocabulary topics

Again, this is not an exhaustive list. Many activities can be adapted to a wide variety of vocabulary topics.

Titles in the Resource Books for Teachers series

Primary Resource Books